MW00607736

Joplin's
CONNOR HOTEL

Joplin's
CONNOR HOTEL

To Ellen:
I hope you enjoy the story of the
Connor,
Chad Stebbins
2-27-21

CHAD STEBBINS

Foreword by Brad Belk, Community Historian

THE
History
PRESS

Published by The History Press
Charleston, SC
www.historypress.com

Copyright © 2021 by Chad Stebbins
All rights reserved

Front cover: Standing on the northwest corner of Fourth and Main, the Connor Hotel was a symbol of Joplin's mining prosperity and known throughout the Midwest for its splendor. *Joplin Historical & Mineral Museum.*

Back cover: Painting of the Connor Hotel lobby by Andy Thomas, a professional artist who works from his studio in Carthage, Missouri.

First published 2021

Manufactured in the United States

ISBN 9781467147675

Library of Congress Control Number: 2020945764

Notice: The information in this book is true and complete to the best of our knowledge. It is offered without guarantee on the part of the author or The History Press. The author and The History Press disclaim all liability in connection with the use of this book.

All rights reserved. No part of this book may be reproduced or transmitted in any form whatsoever without prior written permission from the publisher except in the case of brief quotations embodied in critical articles and reviews.

CONTENTS

FOREWORD

Buildings define us as a civilization. They describe, explain and visually connect us to the past.

The geographical concentration of commercial businesses, along with the inflation of land values, forced architects to design upward toward the sky. Coupled with manufactured steel skeleton frames and the elevator, multi-story hotels became an integral part of the American downtown landscape.

No building in Joplin, Missouri, stood grander than the Connor Hotel. This once-proud landmark was a civic monument—a center of communal life where a lifetime of special memories were nostalgically savored.

Joplin's Connor Hotel is more than just the story of a hotel. The Connor Hotel's legend revealed the city's character, mirroring the social history of Joplin. Dr. Chad Stebbins has generously shared and creatively sprinkled local, regional and state history throughout his book. It is a remarkable look at eight meaningful decades from Joplin's past.

Dr. Stebbins has done an extraordinary job documenting the most iconic twentieth-century structure in southwest Missouri. His research is impeccable, and his use of primary sources is extremely thorough. Most importantly, he has further illuminated the importance of the daily newspapers that chronicle everyday life. Recently, progressive steps have been made in accessing this comprehensive resource via the computer. Today, history is at our fingertips. The long, tedious days spent staring at microfilm are finally over.

Most of us want things to remain the same and are reluctant to change. We slip into a world of false security, carelessly taking for granted that our precious buildings will remain intact—that is, until they are razed. Then, in time, our memories begin to fade and blur as we lose perspective because no tangible touchpoint is left. How do we explain the past building fabric to future generations when there is nothing remaining to point out? The building that once was there becomes nothing more than a footnote to history, representing a far distant reference in time.

The Connor Hotel also exposes a myth of the National Register of Historic Places designation. In 1973, the Connor received its most distinguished honor when the building was placed in the National Register. All the National Register's designations are henceforth eternal listings. Unfortunately, the buildings are not. Having received the highest honor a structure or site can acquire sadly does not guarantee protection forever. Thus, some of America's greatest buildings will continue to be demolished regardless of the honors they so richly deserve. This is preciously why both the written and visual historical recordings of these amazing edifices are imperative.

Although there was no happy ending to the tragic demise of the Connor Hotel, there is tremendous value in recording the entire story. Through Dr. Stebbins's images and narrative, the Connor Hotel is brought back to life.

Chad, we thank you for allowing us to relive the past—to step back in time and get one more glimpse at the golden age of the Connor Hotel. Your historical manuscript teaches us to never forget the value of our yesteryears, and for that, we are forever grateful.

BRAD BELK
Community Historian, Missouri Southern State University
Director and Curator, Joplin Historical Neighborhoods Inc.
Director Emeritus, Joplin Historical & Mineral Museums Inc.

ACKNOWLEDGEMENTS

Since becoming executive director of the Joplin Historical & Mineral Museum in 1987, Brad Belk has been his hometown's top promoter of local history. He also served as my personal cheerleader on this book, encouraging me every step of the way. His frequent question—"When will it be done?"—always inspired me to work just a little harder. Brad also believed that the Connor Hotel was worthy of a book and promoted it before he had even read a single word.

There were many others who helped along the way. Kayla Reed, MSSU's access services librarian, secured several books and articles through interlibrary loan. Chris Wiseman, who succeeded Brad as director of the Joplin Museum Complex, scanned in about half of the photos for this book and was particularly helpful. Bill Caldwell, the "retired" librarian at the *Joplin Globe*, provided several others from the newspaper's archives. Bill began writing a local history column in the *Globe* on Sundays in January 2016.

As a senior at Memorial High School in Joplin when the Connor collapsed in 1978, Greg Holmes took some priceless photos just before and after the disaster. Greg wisely saved all his negatives all these years and made them available to me. Graphic artist Carl Fowler did quite a bit of photo scanning and touching up, and I highly recommend him if you need anything of the sort or something designed. Dr. David Locher, a professor of sociology at MSSU, was terrific at pinpointing when a particular photo was taken based on the make and model of visible cars.

Jill Halback Sullivan, executive director of the Post Art Library, was the one who recommended The History Press as a potential publisher for this book. Jill is certainly doing her part to help tell the story of Joplin's past. She also provided numerous photos from the Joplin Public Library. Retired MSSU history professor Gingy Laas and Carolyn Trout, retired head librarian of the Joplin Public Library, were also very supportive, as was my boss at MSSU, Dr. Paula Carson, provost. Dr. Brad Hodson, MSSU's executive vice-president, has been interested in this book because of his vision in turning the former public library building—where the Connor stood—into a downtown campus for the university.

My eldest son, Brennan, who shares my love of local history, edited the manuscript and made some valuable suggestions. My wife, Laurel, graciously allowed me to spend hundreds of hours on this project while there was much work to be done around the house and outside.

Good friend Gary Sosniecki, who went through the publication process a few months before me, helped to inspire me to complete the long journey. Dr. Conrad Gubera, the longest-serving faculty member in MSSU history, reviewed the introduction to this book on a trip to Cuba in 2017 and made some helpful suggestions.

Chad Rhoad, senior acquisitions editor at The History Press, was extremely easy to work with and seemingly answered every one of my numerous questions within a matter of minutes. Ryan Finn, senior editor, did a masterful job of editing the book and made several corrections for grammar, style, spelling and consistency.

Finally, this book wouldn't have been possible without the excellent coverage of the Connor Hotel by the *Joplin Globe* and *News Herald* over a seventy-year period. Those reporters did a marvelous job of documenting seemingly every facet of the Grand Old Lady's fascinating story.

THE PLACE TO BE

Charles Schifferdecker could hardly contain his excitement the night the Connor Hotel opened in Joplin, Missouri, on Sunday, April 12, 1908. Determined to be the bar's first customer when it flung open its doors at midnight, Joplin's wealthiest citizen ordered a drink and handed catering manager Charles Renner a $1,000 bill. It took Renner a moment to realize that Schifferdecker wanted no change back for his G, that the German-born beer baron simply wanted to make his own contribution to Joplin's palatial hotel. The well-traveled Renner, who had served in the First U.S. Volunteer Cavalry (the "Rough Riders") under Colonel Teddy Roosevelt during the Spanish-American War, was equally impressed with his new place of employment. "It is too fine a hotel for Joplin; it should be in Chicago," he told his boss that evening.

The unveiling of the eight-story hotel—nine floors including the rooftop—was the social event of 1908, perhaps of the entire "aughts" decade. The Connor formally opened with a dinner at 6:00 p.m. Sunday, attended by "handsomely gowned women with waving plumes on their hats" and a large number of men in evening dress. Some 350 guests were served while an orchestra played; another 200 were turned away. While the well-heeled ate, hundreds more peered at them from the street through the dining room's large bay windows. Diners who arrived early received larger portions than those who came through later in the evening; the hotel didn't expect so many guests and had to shrink the serving sizes to stretch the food. "I didn't know Joplin people were such big eaters," said an employee two days later.

After nearly two years of construction, the Connor Hotel finally opened its doors on April 12, 1908. *Joplin Historical Postcards/Joplin Public Library.*

Sightseers converged on the Connor all Sunday afternoon and evening (the hotel was closed during the evening dinner). Employees estimated that between three and four thousand traipsed through on self-guided tours, inspecting every nook and cranny of the million-dollar hotel. Although children had to be accompanied by their parents, everyone was allowed to roam freely, from room to room and floor to floor. Upon reaching the Roof Garden, the crowds had a commanding view of the city of Joplin.

"The crowd which welcomed us today was certainly a great surprise and was not expected," said D.J. Dean, who along with his brother, A.J., had signed a lease to operate the hotel. "I had no idea that the people would throng to the hotel for dinner in nearly as large crowds as they did, and I can tell you that to the business men who are starting in on a new venture, it is certainly a great thing to be welcomed like this."

The Dean brothers, of Kansas City, had almost decided against letting the public have free rein of the building. A torrential downpour two days earlier had caused the Willow Branch—a large creek running underground around Main and Joplin Streets—to overflow, filling basements of businesses along Main Street and causing "general demoralization." The Deans were afraid the public would muddy the carpets and rugs made of foreign weaves and considered making only the lobby and other tiled rooms available for their inspection. A clear day, however, and the desire to show off "the most magnificent hotel that has ever been erected, in the history of the world, in a city of this size" caused them to stick with their original plans.

It was an auspicious beginning to an edifice that would quickly become Joplin's center of the universe for the next fifty years. For decades, most distances were measured from the Connor: a bungalow for sale was a five-minute walk from the hotel, a chicken and berry farm was twenty-seven blocks away, an eighty-acre farm was nine miles north on Highway 43 and a thirty-acre lot had a "fine view of Connor hotel." The Grand Old Lady was also the reference point for height comparisons; even in the 1960s, the manager of the Rocketdyne plant at Neosho was referring to the Saturn missile as standing "about 15 or 16 stories tall, almost twice the height of the Connor hotel."

Until the fourteen-story Messenger Towers opened in 1975, the Connor Hotel was the tallest building in Joplin. As such, it attracted more than its share of hustlers and daredevils. Alvin "Titanic" Thompson, who traveled around the area wagering on anything and everything, won several bets by throwing a lime, an orange, a pumpkin and a walnut over the roof. At least five "human flies" or "human spiders" scaled the hotel between 1915 and 1920.

At the Connor, you could watch the world go by—celebrities, politicians, famous athletes, traveling salesmen, fugitives, con men and swindlers—or at least you could watch Joplin go by. Every social event of any consequence was held there: weddings, rehearsal dinners, receptions, banquets, dances and balls, recitals, club meetings, dinner parties, luncheons and the St. Avips Ball in the 1960s. The hotel's lobby was the town square, or at least the living room, of the burgeoning community. "Chair warmers" or "lobby loungers" were seemingly always present to catch up on the latest gossip. Countless mining deals were consummated at the cigar stand or in the Connor bar as the mining kings smoked Havanas or swilled Waterfill & Frazier bourbon until Prohibition closed the saloon in 1919.

The Connor was in a class by itself when it came to elegance and extravagance. One of its early chefs, Jacques Jaquin, arrived from Chambéry, France, by way of the Waldorf Astoria and Delmonico's in New York. Jaquin created elaborate dishes that tickled the imagination as well as the palate. Guests at a 1911 New Year's Eve dinner were mesmerized by a snowy castle and mountain scene, a succulent pig, a "magnificent fish resting on oysters," seashells gracing the center of the table and carnations and roses in ample supply. The hotel was even known to ship in giant tortoises by rail from the East Coast so diners could feast on turtle soup.

How many hotels in the Midwest had their own orchestra? The Connor did, directed for many years by Professor Victor Kreyer. It also boasted that it was the first hotel in the United States to publish its own newspaper, in 1913. Copies of *Atop the Connor Bulletin* reportedly were sent to "every hotel of importance in the west."

The Connor was known for its fabulous Rooftop Garden, nine stories above the ground, where guests could enjoy the evening's "cool breezes that can always be found at such an altitude." The formal opening of the garden in August 1912 drew 1,500 guests; an elevator carried 10 people up and 10 people down in ninety seconds. Amenities included a restroom for women, a lavatory for men (with a telephone!), a high railing around the roof so that no one would fall off, the regular Connor orchestra and, of course, a "big supply of fresh air and the superb view of the stars and city."

Atop the Connor was the place to be for anyone wanting a night out. Large crowds enjoyed "light and frivolous entertainment," and by the summer of 1913, Joplin had gone "cabaret wild." According to the *Joplin News Herald*, "There is no let-up to the show, beginning at 7:30, and it goes on right through with a whoop until midnight."

Bob Cummings, arguably Joplin's most famous actor along with Dennis Weaver, likened the Roof Garden to the one gracing New York's Waldorf Astoria when he was in high school. "I probably fell in and out of love with at least twenty-five girls up here," he recalled more than thirty years later.

Other cities looked on in envy. In a 1912 editorial titled "Columbia Needs a 'Connor,'" the *Columbia Missourian* lamented the fact that the city did not have a "good hotel" to accommodate its most "critical" visitors. The *Missourian* claimed that the Connor provided the best hotel service in southwest Missouri and served as an advertisement for the city: "It has made Joplin one of the most popular convention cities in the state. No traveling man or other visitor who is within twenty or thirty miles of Joplin will spend the night anywhere else if he can manage to get to the Connor. This is the kind of a hotel Columbia needs."

The editor of the *Chanute (KS) Daily Tribune* also saw the Connor as "Joplin's biggest advertisement." After visiting the hotel during a 1913 newspaper convention, he observed that "[f]rom whatever point of the compass you approach this great mining town, the first object to greet your eye is this fine hostelry that would be a credit to any metropolis.…Verily, the town that has a Connor is on the highway to prosperity and greatness."

Thanks to the Connor Hotel—and the network of railways serving the city—Joplin became a leading convention destination soon after the hotel opened. Joplin quickly billed itself as the "Convention City of the Southwest," and conventioneers poured into the city for the next fifty years. After a nine-story annex to the Connor was completed in 1929, the hotel could accommodate more than one thousand guests at a time if two or three people stayed in each of its four hundred rooms.

For seventy years, the famous Joplin hostelry towered over the city. There were other notable buildings in the city's history—the Keystone Hotel, the Joplin Union Depot, the Newman Building, the Frisco Building, Memorial Hall and more—but all paled in comparison to the economic and social impact the Connor had. Lead and zinc mining may have put Joplin on the map, but the hotel kept it there and made it seem like more of a cosmopolitan city to local residents and to the rest of the nation.

THE BUILDING OF A HOTEL

By the turn of the century, Joplin had become a boomtown of staggering proportions. Its population had jumped from 9,943 in 1890 to 26,023 in 1900, a 162 percent increase. A *St. Louis Post-Dispatch* correspondent who visited the city noted its broad streets, fine buildings, street railways and electric lights, as well as the fact that it had five banks—none of which had ever failed. "The streets are filled with vehicles from morning till night; the electric cars have no vacant seats; the sidewalks are thronged; the shops are too small for the purchasers," he further described.

Another correspondent, from the *Sedalia Weekly Sentinel*, expressed "astonishment" over his visit to southwest Missouri. "Joplin and Webb City are on a boom. Zinc and lead are found in abundance. Everything is on the jump. All branches of trade are represented there, and are flourishing." He did issue a warning to other visitors: "Hit Joplin early in the morning or you may have to sleep in the street that night."

Joplin's prosperity did produce an extreme housing and hotel shortage. Miners, speculators and investors flocked to the city and often found themselves living in tents or tiny shacks. The *St. Louis Post-Dispatch* correspondent who came in May 1899 summed it up: "After every train comes in the hotelkeepers throw up their hands in despair. Every room is taken steadily; every one that will hold two beds has them. Men register and await the departures of guests to take their turns for chances at rooms. The registers always show a 'waiting' list. There are no rooms to rent in town.

Joplin was the heart of the Tri-State District, the heaviest producer of lead and zinc in the world. The district included southeastern Kansas, northeastern Oklahoma and southwestern Missouri. *T.W. Osterloh postcard.*

There are no houses to rent in town. Building is going on all the time. The biggest hotel in town, six stories high—the one where the head waiter wears his gorgeous evening clothes at high noon, is doubling its capacity. And the town is only twenty-five years old!"

The correspondent referenced the Keystone Hotel, which sat on the southeast corner of Fourth and Main. In 1888, a newspaper publisher from Harrisburg, Pennsylvania, named E.Z. Wallower purchased the site for $16,000—the highest price ever paid for a piece of land in Joplin at the time. Regarded as the "palace hotel of the Southwest" when it opened in 1892, the six-story Keystone boasted Joplin's first elevator and the fact that it sat at the junction of all the electric car lines in the city. Wallower added a four-story annex in 1899, making it an entire block long, from Main Street to Virginia Avenue along Fourth Street, and for a while the Keystone claimed that it was the longest hotel in the state.

The other major hotel was aptly named the Joplin Hotel. Opened to great fanfare on July 4, 1874, at the northwest corner of Fourth and Main, the three-story hotel quickly became known as "one of the finest west of St. Louis." It had fifty guest rooms, a spacious office, a dining room that measured fifty feet long by forty feet wide, several large "sample rooms" where clothing salesmen could show their products, baggage rooms and "richly furnished parlors." The guest rooms were "well arranged and ventilated" and had gas lights and nearby fire escapes. Also known as the "Brick Hotel," it was

Built in 1892, the six-story Keystone Hotel dominated the Joplin skyline until eclipsed by the Connor Hotel. *Joplin Historical Postcards/Joplin Public Library.*

built for about $46,000—including some $30,000 in furnishings—by Patrick Murphy, William P. Davis, Elliot R. Moffet and John B. Sergeant, who made up the Joplin Hotel Company.

Thomas Connor, Joplin's millionaire zinc king, bought half of the Joplin Hotel for $6,500 in 1881. Thomas Jones, the other co-owner, also served as manager. The Joplin Hotel, which quickly became the hub of the city's political and social scene, placed armchairs in front of the Main Street side to entice visitors to enter. The chairs were often occupied by the mining kings, who puffed on fat cigars while discussing the latest lead and zinc strikes.

Although born in Ireland, Tom Connor lived the classic American rags-to-riches story. Described as a "self-made man," he seemed to have the Midas touch, especially when it came to buying acreage that contained enormous rich lead and zinc deposits. Connor never sank a shaft, drilled a hole, physically worked a mine or struck zinc ore himself. Instead, he simply acquired the land and leased it to prospectors.

The *St. Louis Post-Dispatch* declared in 1899 that Connor owned "more property than he can keep track of." Another newspaper estimated that he owned about 6,000 acres of mineral land—2,500 in Jasper County, 3,000 in Newton County and 500 near Galena, Kansas. According to one account, he was earning $10,000 per week from mining royalties, enough to earn him the unofficial title of Joplin's first millionaire.

Although he disliked the mining baron, Wallower agreed to a proposal from Connor and Jones in the 1890s to split the earnings of the Joplin Hotel and the Keystone and share a single manager. "For the first few years the earnings of the Joplin Hotel were larger, but toward the close of the [five-year] contract the Keystone was ahead," Wallower wrote in his autobiography. "A second contract for five years was entered into, with the result that the Joplin Hotel was a continual loss, which the Keystone had to make good, and then divide the balance of its earnings."

Early in the new century, Wallower informed Connor that he would not renew the ten-year agreement to split the proceeds and share a manager. Much to the Pennsylvanian's astonishment, Connor said it didn't matter—that he would be building a brand-new $250,000 hotel. Wallower, naturally, was skeptical. "Tom Connor had never done anything for the city, and I therefore regarded his statement as to the erection of a new hotel as a bluff," he recalled years later.

Initially, Connor *was* bluffing. He had planned to remodel and modernize the old Joplin Hotel while adding a fourth floor and installing elevators. Several "progressive citizens" appealed to him, however, to tear down the thirty-year-old structure and build a modern, up-to-date hotel that would serve the booming city well into the new century. But first, Tom had to acquire sole ownership of the Joplin Hotel. He and Jones had had a "quarrel" and were no longer friends. Connor brought a partition suit against the co-owner, forcing the property, furniture and fixtures to be sold at a public auction.

The three-story Joplin Hotel opened in 1874 on the northwest corner of Fourth and Main—the future site of the Connor Hotel. *Joplin Historical & Mineral Museum.*

A large crowd gathered at the Joplin courthouse on Thursday afternoon, January 4, 1906, as the agents for two unidentified buyers engaged in a spirited bidding war. It was widely assumed that the agents represented Connor and Jones, but there was also speculation that Alfred H. Rogers (president of the Southwest Missouri Railroad Company) and Wallower were involved rather than Jones. Rogers was present at the auction, having arrived by special train the day before. The onlookers gasped as the price reached $100,000 and continued to climb. Finally, one agent declined to go any higher, and the sheriff announced, "Sold, to the Connor Realty Company, for $104,500." Jones, who walked away with half the amount (more than $1 million today), was obviously quite pleased with the outcome.

A week after the auction, twenty-six Joplin community leaders and ten businesses quietly signed an agreement to pledge $41,450 to Tom as a "bonus or remuneration" if he would tear down the old Joplin Hotel and build a modern, fireproof hotel "not less than six stories high" on the same site. The "subscription" was quite specific: 10 percent would be paid when he accepted the agreement, 10 percent when a contract was signed with a builder, 10 percent when the basement was completed, 20 percent when

Left: Thomas Connor (1847–1907) seemed to have the Midas touch, especially when it came to buying land that contained enormous lead and zinc deposits. *Joplin Historical & Mineral Museum.*

Right: E.Z. Wallower (1854–1941), a newspaper publisher from Harrisburg, Pennsylvania, bought the "best corner in the city," the southeast corner of Fourth and Main, to build the Keystone Hotel. *Joplin Historical & Mineral Museum.*

the building was four stories high, 25 percent when the building was under a roof and the balance, 25 percent, when the building was completed and ready for occupancy.

Gilbert Barbee, a Democratic political leader of southwest Missouri, gave $3,000. So did Leonidas "Lon" P. Cunningham, a mine owner and attorney. A banker, Howard C. Murphy, offered $2,500; he was the son of the late Patrick Murphy (founder of Murphysburg, which was incorporated into the city of Joplin in 1873). Also pledging $2,500 was James "Jimmy" Worth, an eccentric Joplin character who owned the Worth Block on the northeast corner of Fourth and Main. Charles Schifferdecker, philanthropist and former president of First National Bank of Joplin, offered $2,000, and so did the Dieter & Wenzel Construction Company.

After one month of speculation and rumor, Connor formally announced his plans on February 10, 1906. "I have determined to give Joplin the finest hotel property in this part of the country," he told a *Joplin News Herald* reporter. "It will be 125 feet on Main street by 110 feet on Fourth, and will be six stories high. No pains will be spared in making the finest hostelry in the Southwest." The *Joplin Daily Globe* reported that the two-hundred-room hotel would cost between $400,000 and $450,000.

Connor had to delay making the announcement until he could acquire the next-door McCarty Drug Store property, owned by a man named Bert McCullough, who was reluctant to sell. Fortunately, Barbee was able to convince McCullough that no one individual should stand in the way of progress. McCullough pocketed $20,000 for the tiny twenty-two-foot frontage at 316 Main, the second-highest price ever paid for real estate in Joplin. He used the proceeds to buy half of the House of Lords saloon across the street.

Next, Connor was ready to select and hire the architects to design his new hotel. His many trips to St. Louis to visit his wife, Melissa, at St. Vincent's Asylum had brought him into contact with Barnett, Haynes & Barnett, the city's leading firm. It was a real coup for Connor to land these architects, known for their opulent creations; just two years earlier, they had been selected to design the gargantuan Palace of Fine Arts at the St. Louis World's Fair. They also drew the plans for the twelve-story, 450-room Hotel Jefferson, which opened in April 1904, just in time to house visitors to the fair.

George Dennis Barnett and his brother-in-law, John Ignatius Haynes, organized an architectural firm in 1889 and were joined by George's younger brother, Thomas P., five years later. George and Tom were the sons of George I. Barnett (1815–1898), an Englishman often regarded as the "dean of St. Louis architects." Barnett Sr. designed the Missouri Governor's Mansion and many of the structures in the Missouri Botanical Garden and Tower Grove Park; he also had a hand in designing the Old Courthouse in St. Louis.

Barnett, Haynes & Barnett designed the Rockcliffe Mansion (1898–1900) and Mark Twain Hotel in Hannibal (1905), as well as the Missouri Athletic Club (1903), the ten-story St. Louis Star building (1903) and the ten-story Marquette Hotel (1906), all in their hometown. After the Connor Hotel, they would go on to design the eighteen-story 1 Wall Street office building in New York (1907), the twelve-story Illinois Athletic Club on Michigan Avenue in Chicago (1908) and the magnificent Cathedral Basilica of St. Louis (1907–14). Adolphus Busch, the cofounder of Anheuser-Busch, later commissioned Tom Barnett to design the twenty-story Adolphus Hotel in Dallas.

Haynes made his first visit to Joplin on February 16, 1906, and spent the better part of the day with Connor. Tom showed him the location for the new Joplin Hotel, and Haynes said it would be a relatively easy task to build a magnificent structure with the dimensions of 125 feet on Main Street and 110 feet along Fourth Street. Tom particularly liked Haynes's idea that the lobby feature a large rotunda, to give the hotel a metropolitan feel.

Connor spent an entire week in St. Louis hammering out the details with Barnett, Haynes & Barnett. Although Joplin residents expected a splendid new hotel, they surely didn't anticipate all the extravagances contained in the description released to the public on March 18. To be designed in a modern French style, the nine-story, $500,000 hotel would feature beautiful bay windows and balconies, a French dining room and Italian garden café, a grand stairway in the center of a large rotunda with marble flooring, a barbershop and billiards room in the basement along with spacious toilet compartments for gentlemen, two high-speed electric passenger elevators and a large service elevator, large compartments for conventions and banquets, sample rooms for use by traveling salesmen, a private bath in all 250 guest rooms with porcelain iron bathtubs and porcelain lavatories and thermostatic heat regulators and local and long-distance telephone service in every room. "This building, when completed, will be the handsomest hotel building west of New York city," the architects declared.

The next step was to put the construction contract out for bid. Joplin citizens felt a measure of pride in May when the local firm of Dieter & Wenzel was awarded the $350,000 contract, beating out a dozen contractors from Chicago, St. Louis, Kansas City and other places. Captain C.A. Dieter and his partner, John Wenzel, had recently completed the four-story Miners Bank at Fourth and Joplin, regarded at the time as the finest building in the city. They had built the Carnegie libraries in Joplin and Carthage and the Joplin Elks Club and were working on the Olivia Apartments and St. Peter's Catholic Church in 1906.

Connor later revealed that he had awarded the contract to the Joplin contractors even though their bid was not the lowest one. "I awarded the contract to Dieter & Wenzel on account of the fact that they were home contractors and employed nothing but home labor, when I could have let the contract to another firm for $5,000 less money," he told the *Webb City Register*. "But Dieter & Wenzel, as I understand it, had built a large number of the big buildings in Joplin, and had always employed home labor and had never had any labor troubles of any kind with their men."

Born in Germany in 1859, "Cap" Dieter learned the building trade as an apprentice in Frankfurt. He moved to the United States and settled in Wichita, opening a construction office at the ripe old age of twenty. He later met Wenzel, who served an apprenticeship under him and became his partner. Dieter came to Joplin in 1900 to supervise the masonry work on the Busch office building at 410 Main and made the city his home until his death thirty years later. Wenzel remained in Joplin until 1910, when he returned to Wichita to open a branch office. The Dieter & Wenzel Construction Company dissolved in 1917, when the C.A. Dieter Construction Company was established.

The plumbing and heating contract went to another hometown bidder, John W. Comerford, who like Dieter & Wenzel beat out competitors from Chicago, St. Louis and Kansas City. Comerford, a New Yorker, had moved to Joplin in 1892 and worked with Connor when Tom was president and chief owner of the Joplin Water Works Company. Comerford had completed contracts at the new government building on Joplin Street and the Clarketon Hotel on Main Street and an estimated one thousand jobs in private residences.

The son-in-law of mining capitalist Edward Zelleken, Comerford surely had no idea of the job ahead of him. Ten carloads of plumbing and six carloads of heating materials would be required to equip the building. Comerford and his crew would have to plumb 125 bathrooms, 250 wash basins and 145 toilet rooms, plus public toilets on every floor. An immense tank on the roof would provide the water supply, and a 1,500-gallon storage tank in the boiler room, heated by copper coils, would furnish hot water instantly to any room in the building. The hotel would have 345 steam radiators and several miles of pipe. The *Joplin Daily Globe* declared that Comerford "will unquestionably establish a record in the installation of plumbing and heating systems which are seldom equaled."

The nine-story building—a semi-skyscraper—would require a staggering amount of steel and brick. It had already been determined that "not a particle of the material" from the old Joplin Hotel would be reused, even though much of the stone and brick was still in excellent condition. (According to the contract, Dieter & Wenzel could sell off any salvage after razing the building.) The contractors spent several days calculating all the materials that would be needed: fifty carloads (one thousand tons) of steel shipped from Pennsylvania, 2 million bricks, forty carloads of cement, two carloads of copper and sheet metal, twenty-five carloads of limestone, one hundred carloads of tailings and fifteen carloads of lumber. Most of the lumber was for falsework, or temporary support structures, and would not be a part of the permanent construction.

The *Joplin Daily Globe* and the *Joplin News Herald* both reported on May 22, 1906, that the new hotel would be called The Katherine, in honor of

Connor's mother, who had died fifteen years earlier. The name didn't stick, however, and it was still called the "new Joplin Hotel" for the next year.

Before a new structure could be built, two others had to be torn down. The first to go was the old McCarty building at 316 Main. The situation at the still-functioning Joplin Hotel was a bit more complicated. In order to bring in some revenue during the expected eleven months of construction, Connor had decided that a forty-room annex to the hotel at 319 Joplin would house guests, and a large room there would be converted into a dining room.

After serving dinner on Saturday evening, June 9, the dining room closed, and all the rooms were stripped bare of furnishings and fittings. An "army of workers" began attacking the building at 7:00 a.m. Monday, and soon a large crowd had gathered to watch. As the roof was being removed, a few onlookers speculated how long it would take to raze the structure—with most thinking somewhere between two weeks and two months.

Dieter & Wenzel used long wooden chutes extending from the third floor to the ground to send brick, wood and rubbish to wagons waiting on the street. Some 600,000 bricks were salvaged, of which 330,000 were judged

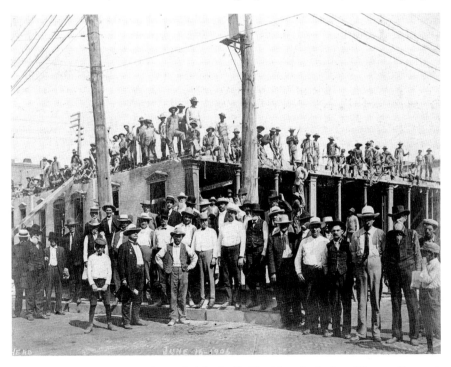

The "army of workers" that dismantled the Joplin Hotel in only six days. Thomas Connor is in the front row, with a rolled-up newspaper in his hand. *Joplin Historical & Mineral Museum.*

to be in fairly good condition. The woodwork from the rooms—all of it oak and in good condition—was taken away to be cleaned for use in other buildings. At least 13 carloads of lumber were also removed. Although more than 750 wagonloads of refuse were hauled away to be used as filler at a place on North Main Street, every door and window lintel, joist, stud and lath was carefully preserved. Despite a constant cloud of dust created by the plastering and debris going down the chutes, the crowds remained throughout the week. By Saturday evening—exactly one week after the "last supper" served in the old dining room—nothing remained standing. The construction company, using ninety-five men, claimed that it had set a world record by demolishing the old Joplin Hotel in only six working days.

The contractors also had an aggressive plan to excavate the basement and create the foundation of the new hotel. Two crews, one working during the day and the other at night, would dig a basement slightly more than ten feet deep and the necessary holes for the stone piers. Arc lights were installed at Fourth and Main so that for the first time in Joplin construction history, twice as much work could be done in a single day.

Joplin's building boom created a skilled labor shortage in the summer of 1906. Other projects underway included the Olivia Apartments, St. Peter's Catholic Church, St. Philip's Episcopal Church, Keller Wagon Factory, Joplin Candy and Specialty Company, Cunningham building, the city hall and fire department and numerous private residences. Unskilled laborers were available, but the building trades experts could have their choice of jobs.

Even the millionaire James "Jimmy" Worth, one of Connor's best friends, helped shovel out the basement while Dieter was in need of men. The fifty-six-year-old owner of the Worth Block across the street donned overalls and swung a pick and shovel for a week. According to the *News Herald*, he "handled a shovel like a veteran and established a record for the amount of work done in a given time."

Shovelers found some pieces of zinc ore at a depth of around five feet. It wasn't completely unexpected, as the men had often said, "It would be Connor's luck to run onto a bunch of lead while digging the cellar to his hotel." The discovery reminded everyone that some of the best mines in the district had been located at what was now Fourth and Main. Mining tunnels, or drifts, still remained under the streets and some of the buildings, including the Keystone Hotel.

Nine stories and 130 feet tall when completed, the new hotel would barely qualify as a skyscraper. But the world's first skyscraper, the Home Insurance

Shovelers excavating the basement of the new hotel on July 1, 1906. *Joplin Historical & Mineral Museum.*

Building in Chicago, was only ten stories and 138 feet. As Joplin residents eagerly anticipated their first steel-frame high-rise, a story in the *Globe* that summer eerily foretold of the accompanying dangers. Under the double-deck banner headline "Joplin to Witness the Perilous Feats of Steel Workers on Skyscrapers," readers were warned that the project might result in a few fatalities.

"From the very beginning of its erection the steel frame of a skyscraper is a dangerous place upon which to work," the article noted. "Even when the work is on the ground level, from three to half a dozen derricks are constantly swinging great steel columns and girders, which weigh anywhere from 500 to 2,000 pounds. The breaking of a cable, the slipping of a pulley, a wrong signal from a derrick foreman, and one of these great beams may crush the life out of a dozen men. Even should one strike a man in swinging about, it might easily kill him or at least injure him seriously."

Sure enough, a cable did break three months later, instantly killing twenty-two-year-old Alva Hively of Marion, Indiana. Hively was a professional girder rider employed by the Des Moines Bridge and Steel Company, a subcontractor hired to erect the steel. Girder riding was perhaps the most dangerous job in the construction business. The rider would balance a steel beam and perform a task known as "spotting"—signaling to the engineer below when the beam was directly over the desired spot and the crane could lower it into place. Large crowds had gathered to watch Hively "riding the boom" the three weeks he had been in Joplin.

The hotel construction site presented a unique challenge to the Des Moines Bridge and Steel Company with all the surrounding telephone lines and cables. The five-thousand-pound steel beams were stacked near Fourth Street and had to be hoisted by a ninety-foot-long crane. Hively first had to make sure that they cleared all the wires before they could be moved into position. Shortly after lunch on Wednesday, September 26, 1906, he was riding a girder about ten feet above the wires when the cable holding it snapped. He fell head first and struck another girder, cutting a deep hole in the back of his skull. He died instantly.

Hively's coworkers had been concerned about the cable for a few days. Five-eighths of an inch in diameter, it was supposed to withstand a lifting strain of twenty-five tons. But it had been burned earlier after touching the electric line that ran over the center of Fourth Street.

When the cable broke, it snapped with such force that the loose end whipped across the street and sliced through the wall of the Club Saloon on the southwest corner of Fourth and Main. The *Joplin Globe* reported that "in some places [it] looks as if it had been cut by a sharp saw." When the crane collapsed, several telephone poles were demolished, and the streets were soon full of live wires. It took several hours before order could be restored to the corner.

The hotel claimed its second fatality a few weeks later when Irvin Neyhard, a forty-one-year-old plumber's helper working for Comerford, plunged four stories to his death. Neyhard either had been standing on or carrying a stepladder on the stairway of the fourth floor leading to the fifth floor when he apparently became dizzy and fell backward. Neyhard's "pitiful scream" followed by the crack of splintering wood got the attention of his coworkers, but they could only watch in horror as he hit the ground. "He was waving his hands wildly, as though grabbing for something to stop him," reported an eyewitness.

The deaths of Hively and Neyhard, tragic as they were, paled in comparison to the one that occurred on March 29, 1907. This one brought a "pall of gloom" upon the entire city of Joplin.

The construction scene on October 1, 1906, five days after the death of Alva Hively. *Joplin Historical & Mineral Museum.*

The news came from San Antonio. The fifty-nine-year-old Connor had died at Dr. Moody's Sanitarium, where he had been a patient since January. Although Moody's was a seventy-five-bed general psychiatric hospital that specialized in nervous and mental diseases, there is little evidence that Tom suffered from such a disorder. He had been elected to the Missouri Senate in November but had not felt well enough to assume office in Jefferson City.

The *Joplin News Herald* reported the afternoon of his death that Connor had suffered "a breakdown caused by the stress of a political campaign and the world of business matters in which he was interested." The *St. Louis Post-Dispatch* said that "overwork" had caused his confinement at the sanitarium and death was due to a cerebral hemorrhage.

The day after his death, the *Joplin Globe* published a front-page editorial suggesting that "The New Joplin Hotel" be called "The Connor Hotel" in Tom's honor. "There is none to protest now against calling the new hotel 'The Connor Hotel,' and wouldn't it be a fitting recognition to do so? Wouldn't it be a handsome thing? Wouldn't it be the right thing to do?"

Meanwhile, construction on the hotel continued. Workers laid the last brick in the walls on May 18, 1907, and the exterior of the hotel pretty much looked as it would for the next two decades except for the missing windows. Dieter & Wenzel now focused on the interior—laying floors, finishing the walls, smoothing the ceilings and completing some stonework.

As the giant hotel towered at Fourth and Main, a *Joplin News Herald* reporter noted that Joplin now had a "flatiron" corner, referencing the wind-tunnel effect created when the Flatiron Building opened in New York five years earlier. The iconic skyscraper's vertical face intensified wind gusts at ground level, blowing men's hats off and raising women's skirts. Joplin residents were also noticing this "downdraught effect" with all the gusty winds around the hotel. "The recent windy days have demonstrated that Joplin has a corner that New York can not excel for breeziness," the reporter observed. "On calm, still days the wind blows in savage gusts around the corner of the new hotel at Fourth and Main and on windy days a veritable hurricane rages up and down Main street and the side streets that lead to Joplin's 'flatiron' corner."

As the community continued to watch everything going on at Fourth and Main with great interest, Connor's heirs made two important announcements on June 11. The hotel officially would be called the Connor Hotel instead of the Joplin Hotel or the New Joplin Hotel, and they had signed a ten-year contract with the Dean brothers of Kansas City to manage it.

In Delevan James (D.J.) Dean and Allen J. (A.J.) Dean, the heirs had selected two of the best-known hotel proprietors in the Midwest. Born in New York, the brothers had succeeded their father in the hotel business. D.J. moved to Kansas in 1887 and operated hotels in Wichita, Pittsburg and Fort Scott. A.J. joined his brother in Pittsburg in 1895 to assist with the Hotel Stilwell, and the brothers soon took charge of the Hotel Savoy while opening the Hotel Baltimore, both in Kansas City. The eleven-story, six-hundred-room Hotel Baltimore, arguably the finest hostelry west of Chicago, served as the headquarters for the 1900 Democratic National Convention.

That the Connor heirs had selected someone else to run their hotel was not unusual. According to Paul Groth in his *Living Downtown: The History of Residential Hotels in the United States*, "As many as nine out of ten owners of large hotels did not personally manage their property. They typically leased the building to a manager for one to ten years." The family would enjoy a steady, fixed income—10 percent of the gross receipts—while the Deans would be responsible for the Connor's profitability.

The hotel appeared to be nearing completion on July 1, 1907, but there was still a considerable amount of work to do inside. *Joplin Historical & Mineral Museum.*

The brothers had the expense of furnishing the new hotel, estimated at $100,000—about $20,000 for the lobby and dining rooms and $400 each for the 210 guest rooms. They would spend another $15,000 on china. "Hotel furniture often belonged to the manager, not the building owner; change of management included the sale of interior furnishings," Groth said.

The Deans wasted no time in insisting on modifications to the plans drawn up by Barnett, Haynes & Barnett, the St. Louis architects. Haynes,

Left: Delevan James (D.J.) Dean. *Right*: Allen J. (A.J.) Dean. *Joplin Historical & Mineral Museum.*

summoned to Joplin by Dieter, agreed that the kitchen could be moved from the eighth floor to the basement. A summer roof garden would replace the mansard roof, or French roof, that had been part of the original plans. Connor had considered the change before his death but had been concerned with the additional cost and the uncertainty of whether a roof garden could sustain interest once the novelty had worn off.

THE JOPLIN SPIRIT

More than two years had passed since the millionaire zinc king had announced his plans to build "the finest hostelry in the Southwest." The Connor was supposed to be ready by April 1907, but now—a year later—Joplinites were getting impatient. The "long-deferred" grand opening finally took place on Sunday, April 12, 1908, when an estimated crowd of three to four thousand did a "thorough inspection" of the million-dollar hotel.

The Connor was even more splendid than anyone could have imagined. Barnett, Haynes & Barnett used a style of architecture known at the time as the modern French school of Renaissance. Today, experts would call it Neoclassical architecture—examples would include Buckingham Palace, the Louvre, the White House, the U.S. Capitol, the Lincoln Memorial and Thomas Jefferson's Monticello.

The hotel's footprint was narrow, 110 feet on Main Street by 120 feet on Fourth Street. The Connor had only two entrances: the main one in front and another in the rear of the building. "I believe that this system will prevent a large amount of thievery," hotel manager O.A. Reif explained to the *Joplin News Herald*. "In many of the city hotels thousands of dollars' worth of articles are lost each year because ample opportunities are offered to persons who care to steal."

The exterior was constructed of Carthage limestone from the quarries of the Spring River Stone Company on the first two floors and granite brick from the Hydraulic Press Brick Company in Kansas City on the other floors.

Except for a sculpted lion's head over the main entrance, two sculpted female faces and some frieze panels on the façades, the hotel wasn't terribly striking on the outside. The architects more than made up for it inside, however.

Guests who came through the Main Street entrance passed under a Roman canopy made of bronze and glass before entering "one of the most spacious and richly ornate lobbies in the United States," according to a promotional brochure that commemorated the hotel's opening. A white Italian marble rotunda and grand staircase was the pièce de résistance. Reportedly costing $250,000, the solid marble staircase had been installed by the St. Louis Marble and Tile Company.

Barnett, Haynes & Barnett used scagliola (plaster imitating marble) to encase the impressive steel structural columns that dominated the rotunda in the center of the building. Leather divans and lounging chairs made the main lobby an inviting place, and the lobby would serve as Joplin's living room for the next fifty or so years.

The ground floor also featured a bar, a cigar and newsstand, writing rooms, a barbershop and three dining rooms: a French dining room, an Italian garden café and a palm room. The *Joplin News Herald*, in a story the day the Connor opened, waxed more enthusiastically about the barbershop than anything else:

> *Nothing so fine in the line of tonsorial apartments has ever been seen in Joplin. The shop is roomy and equipped with seven chairs. The room is finished in white enamel with mahogany trimmings and the chairs are of leather and mahogany. Barbers of the greatest skill have been secured for the hair cutting and shaving department, and patrons of the hotel can rest assured that operations performed upon their physiognomies in the Connor hotel will be delightful, pleasing and soothing, and they will come forth looking and feeling like new men. No expense has been spared to make the equipment of the Connor hotel barber shop up to the standard of that which prevails in the largest metropolitan shops.*

Bert Wagner, who would go on to serve as a municipal judge, ran the barbershop. The seven chairs, of white enamel upholstery in apple green leather, had been ordered from the Theodore A. Kochs Company of Chicago, whose chairs were known for their remarkable craftsmanship. Each station had a spotless porcelain lavatory, and each barber wore white to give the appearance of a clean, sanitary parlor. Nothing could ruin a barbershop's business faster than barber's itch. Caused by infection-ridden

Sculpted lion's head and caryatids over the main entrance. *Joplin Historical & Mineral Museum.*

The entrance featured a Roman canopy, made entirely of bronze and glass. *Joplin Historical & Mineral Museum.*

The Connor claimed that it had one of the most spacious and richly ornate lobbies in the country. The rotunda was finished in white Italian marble, and the grand staircase was built of solid marble. *Joplin Historical Postcards/Joplin Public Library.*

razors or contaminated combs and brushes, barber's itch was similar to eczema, acne and even ringworm. "No BARBERS' ITCH is possible at this sanitary shop," claimed a 1912 Connor ad. "Every instrument that touches the skin is sterilized—the germs simply can't survive."

The basement contained the kitchen, storerooms, a refrigeration system, a power substation, offices for the chefs, toilet rooms and the billiards room. Again, the Deans had spared no expense in making the billiards parlor—consisting of four tables for pool and two for billiards—"the most elaborate pleasure resort of the kind in the city." Because of the kitchen's location in the basement, male help in the dining rooms was a necessity. As the *Joplin News Herald* explained, "Women would not be strong enough to climb the stairs and carry heavy loads of dishes."

The marble staircase led from the lobby to the mezzanine level, branching into a north flight and a south flight of stairs after eighteen steps. A "sumptuously furnished" main drawing room at the head of the stairway would become a favorite lounging place for guests looking for a place to unwind. A large circular opening in the center of this parlor provided a commanding view of the lobby beneath. (A white Venetian railing around the circular opening prevented anyone from suffering a nasty fall.) Private banquet rooms were to the north and, to the west, a private dining room.

A section of the café fronting Main Street. *Joplin Historical & Mineral Museum.*

The Connor had 210 rooms, called guests' apartments or sleeping apartments in 1908. There were no interior rooms; each room had an exterior window. "Every room and corridor has daylight and direct opening to sun and air," boasted the hotel's promotional brochure. Fewer than half the rooms had a private bathroom, but there were "large general toilets" on every floor. According to Paul Groth in his *Living Downtown: The History of Residential Hotels in the United States*, "In hotels of 1910, providing a full bathroom for every room was not yet common. About half the rooms had a private bath, and the rest shared hall bathrooms."

The most novel feature was a switch in the tumbler of the door lock of every room so that the lights were automatically turned on and off when the guest turned the room key upon entering and leaving. The Deans purchased the top-of-the-line Schultz & Hirsch mattresses from Chicago after testing them at the Hotel Baltimore in Kansas City.

The Connor also wowed guests with its high-speed elevators, rugs and carpets made of foreign weave and handsome furniture. The hotel had several large "sample" rooms, where traveling salesmen could display their

From this circular gallery on the second floor, the entire lobby could be viewed. *Joplin Historical & Mineral Museum.*

wares, usually clothing and hats but also shoes, groceries, tobacco, matches and any number of other staples. These salesmen—called "drummers" a hundred years ago—came from New York, Chicago, Detroit, St. Louis and Oklahoma City and would stop at the Connor for a day or two.

Next to the marble staircase, the crown jewel was the rooftop summer garden, the likes of which Joplin had never seen before. "The whole roof comprises a modern and pleasant roof garden, which is sufficiently high up to lend a view of the surrounding country and to make a most delightful retreat," the brochure read. In an ad placed in the *Joplin Globe* the day the Connor opened, the architects pointed out that a row of electric lights extending around the roof gave it a "clear and peculiarly beautiful appearance in the night time."

The Deans brought in at least five of their Kansas City employees to operate the new hotel: O.A. Reif, manager; Sam B. Campbell, chief clerk and assistant manager; Eugene Munger, bar manager; Sam Hobbs, headwaiter; and Charles H. Leach, head porter. The chef, assistant chef, housekeeping supervisor and Campbell's assistant all came from New York.

One of the private bathrooms. *Joplin Historical & Mineral Museum.*

The first banquet at the Connor quite likely was the longest one in the hotel's seventy-year existence. To celebrate the opening of the Joplin Stock Exchange on April 28, 1908, officers and the board of directors planned an eleven-course feast that included fillet of halibut, broiled spring chicken on toast and stuffed tomatoes. Manager Reif, who seated the 150 guests at small round tables instead of at the customary rectangular tables, claimed that it was the first time this arrangement had been used for a large banquet outside of New York.

Following a reception in the lobby, the doors to the main dining room swung open at 9:00 p.m. There were introductions, toasts, speeches and vocal and orchestral performances as the banqueters sipped champagne and puffed on cigarettes and cigars. "Oratory flowed like wine, freely imbibed by Joplinites, whose yearning for compliments to the city was satisfied," reported the *Joplin Daily Globe*. When a storm knocked out the power at midnight and plunged the hotel in darkness, the gala continued by candlelight until shortly after 3:00 a.m.

Missouri secretary of state John E. Swanger gave the most memorable speech of the evening—or morning:

> *Cities are known by their characteristics. New York for its Wall Street, Chicago and Kansas City for their live stock markets, Milwaukee for its malt and Joplin for its lead and zinc. But above this material element of greatness are the pluck, push and purposes of the people who have*

transformed this prairie land by the wand of progress and reared a magnificent city, stamped with a spirit all its own. I greet the Joplin spirit here. It was the Joplin spirit which caused the late Thomas Connor to rear this magnificent hotel which is a credit to Joplin, to Missouri and to the world. The Joplin spirit conquers all things, and in this, your latest undertaking, I believe that adequate expression will be found in the success of the stock exchange.

Before the conventions came, the Connor had to rely on the traveling salesmen for a good portion of its business. But when they left the road for about two weeks during the holidays, the hotel felt the pinch. "Christmas is playing havoc with the hotel business in Joplin," said Campbell, the assistant manager. "Everyone is going home and as a result the number of our guests is reduced to a third of its usual proportions."

To generate more revenue from the hotel's dining rooms, the Deans sent their Belgian-born, French-trained chef to take charge of the Connor's kitchen. Adrian Delvaux had worked at Le Grand Hôtel in Reims and the Bristol Hotel in Paris before becoming chef of the Chicago Club in 1890. After stints with the Congress Hotel and the Auditorium Hotel in Chicago, the Deans brought him to Kansas City in 1903 as chef de cuisine of the Hotel Baltimore.

In his 2017 book, *The Culinarians: Lives and Careers from the First Age of American Fine Dining*, author David S. Shields listed "The Great Adrian" as one of the 175 most influential chefs, caterers and restaurateurs from 1793 to 1919. "When Delvaux walked into the kitchen, the Baltimore had only two rivals west of New York for size and amenities: the Palmer House in Chicago and Brown's Hotel in Denver. Adrian Delvaux knew precisely the opportunity standing before him—an exquisite venue in a city ambitious for commercial and cultural distinction. Delvaux wholeheartedly embraced his role as oracle of the good living."

Connor Hotel guests who participated in Delvaux's 1908 Christmas dinner tickled their palates with the likes of Blue Point oysters, clear green turtle soup, planked whitefish served with sliced cucumbers, boiled Philadelphia capon (a young, castrated rooster) in Chevalier sauce, lamb chops, roast tenderloin of beef, roast suckling pig with apple dressing, roast young turkey, candied sweet potatoes, asparagus seasoned with French vinaigrette, frozen eggnog and English plum pudding. While the temporary posting of such a famous chef brought the hotel some revenue and publicity, its reputation would take a big hit in 1909.

The interior of the legendary House of Lords. The cash register is on display at the Joplin Museum Complex. *Joplin Historical & Mineral Museum.*

That the House of Lords saloon across the street harbored gambling, prostitution and other forms of vice was no secret. Opened in 1892 and named by an Englishman staying at the Keystone Hotel, the establishment advertised that it sold fine wines, liquors and cigars. There was a bar and restaurant on the first floor, gambling rooms on the second floor and "ladies in waiting" on the third floor. The gambling rooms had peepholes and more than a dozen secret doors and entrances, allowing quick exits should the need arise.

A Joplin city ordinance prohibited gambling, but police had little interest in arresting anyone. The House of Lords was the most popular place in town, where you could get a good meal or a stiff drink while listening to the many bands, orchestras and ragtime artists who performed there. But mounting public pressure on the law to act prompted a Monday evening raid in July 1908. While the sheriff and another officer walked through the bar and up the stairway directly into the main gambling room, the assisting prosecuting attorney and a patrolman entered through a side door. To no one's surprise—well, the surprise may have been the number—they found thirty men playing roulette, faro and poker.

As several of the men slipped out through all the doors and entrances, the dealers began collecting the money on the tables. Sheriff's deputies attempted to guard the gambling room and secure the evidence until morning, but the roulette wheel and faro bank somehow disappeared. Fred Firey, the co-proprietor of the gambling den, was the one operating the roulette wheel that night. He and his wheel would soon figure prominently in another case.

A wave of religious revival had been sweeping across Joplin, and hundreds had signed petitions requesting that evangelist Billy Sunday come at the earliest possible date. The Joplin Ministers' Alliance and the Merchants' Association believed that Sunday's appearance in Joplin would result in "the greatest moral awakening the city has ever experienced."

Getting Billy Sunday to come to Joplin would be no small feat. The former Major League Baseball player's schedule often was set two years in advance, and cities hosting him had to build a temporary wooden tabernacle for his revival services. His entourage—a private secretary, a stenographer, four assistant speakers and several singers—had to be accommodated as well, normally costing $1,000 per week.

As a mining town, Joplin overall was more liberal than the religious community and took more of a laissez-faire attitude to gambling. For those wondering what harm it caused, the *Joplin Globe* spelled it out in a lengthy editorial that began on the May 26, 1909 front page. The newspaper referred to the "plunder of hard-working miners" whose weekly wages went into the pockets of professional gamblers instead of buying food for their families.

The *Globe* seemed strangely sympathetic to the House of Lords, pointing out that the owner claimed that if gambling were taking place there, he didn't know anything about it. Instead, the paper referred repeatedly to Mose Miller's "gambling hell" at Fifth and Main. It mentioned a young businessman who was "robbed" at Miller's place; he had been intoxicated and didn't realize that the dice were "fixed" as he lost a lot of money in a craps game.

Responding to the *Globe's* editorial, law enforcement officials that evening conducted a simultaneous raid of the House of Lords, Mose Miller's and Newt Persinger's place in the Worth Building at Fourth and Main. Those who raided Mose Miller's arrested Miller after finding and removing several craps tables. The haul was much bigger at Newt Persinger's: a roulette wheel, three craps tables, poker tables and other gambling devices. Persinger was also arrested.

Guy Humes, who had been elected mayor in April 1909, had been going on a one-man crusade to eliminate Joplin's lawless ways. He raided the House of Lords on a Sunday evening—Halloween—and found ten to twelve men drinking whiskey and beer. Because it was against the law to sell liquor on a Sunday, Humes and two policemen arrested proprietor Bert McCullough and three employees.

"The gamblers will stay away permanently and the saloon keepers will continue to observe the Sunday closing laws so long as I am mayor of Joplin," Humes told a *Kansas City Star* reporter who spent two days in Joplin observing the festering situation.

The reporter painted a vivid description of the House of Lords, calling it "the pioneer saloon, café, pool hall and room housing in Joplin" with "red paint and expensive furnishings." He noted, "It is the headquarters of many of the politicians, and the stronghold of those who do not like to see old conditions disturbed."

Given all the moral decay, turmoil and lawlessness in Joplin, the city needed the type of salvation that only Billy Sunday could deliver. After months of negotiations, he agreed to come for at least five weeks, from November 24, 1909, until just past Christmas. "You may not like what I will say, but I did not beg for the privilege of coming to Joplin," he said upon his arrival. "I was begged to come here. I refused over a hundred cities to come to this place, and I will say what I please."

Sunday's architect and front man, A.P. Gill, arrived three weeks before the baseball evangelist to direct the building of the tabernacle on Virginia Avenue between Fifth and Sixth Streets. Described as a "short, heavy-set man shouting orders in all directions," Gill barely allowed anyone to talk during the four days of construction. Sixty amateur carpenters, which included every pastor in Joplin, used 125,000 feet of lumber and at least twelve kegs of nails in completing the six-thousand-seat structure.

Sunday, who came to Joplin from Cedar Rapids, Iowa, was accompanied by his eight-year-old son, Billy Jr. His wife, Helen, would not arrive until ten days later with their youngest son, Paul. The

Billy Sunday. *Library of Congress.*

Sundays wisely did not stay at the Connor Hotel; instead, they resided in the W.E. Saunders home at 302 Pearl Avenue.

The baseball evangelist didn't waste any time in targeting Joplin's infamous watering hole. On his third night in town, he preached a sermon titled "The Moral Leper" in which he claimed that "Joplin has been run too long by a gang of dirty whiskey-soaked curs." He went on to say, "If a man wants to be a Christian, what will he do? Why, go up here to the House of Lords, and ask some of that gang that loafs around there. That's been the city hall for the past few years, from all I can learn."

Sunday hated all kinds of vice and demoralization but had a particular disdain for those who operated drinking establishments. Time and time again, he railed against them from his revival pulpit. "When are we going to stop putting fine clothes on the backs of the saloon keepers' wives, while our own go around in rags?" he asked. "When will we stop feeding our children on soup bones, like dogs, when we help feed the saloon man on juicy porterhouse steaks?" Sunday estimated that Joplin's saloonkeepers were taking more than $1 million per year out of the pockets of the miners, their wives and children.

His only reference to the name Connor came when he mistakenly referred to the Conqueror Trust Company as the Connor Trust Company. A member of his choir corrected him: "Conqueror, Conqueror." Sunday replied, "Very well, Conqueror then. I thought it was Connor; everything else around this town seems to be Connor."

Sunday would have ample opportunity just a few days later to use the name Connor correctly during his crusade. Under mounting public pressure to clean up the town, Humes led another raid on Sunday evening, December 5, 1909. But this time, the House of Lords wasn't his target—the Connor Hotel was.

Humes had heard rumors of gambling at the Connor for some time, especially since things had quieted down at the saloon across the street. With Humes's permission, Joplin attorney Lee Shepherd hired a man named J.L. Haines (or Haynes), "distinguished by a wild western mustache and steely blue eyes," to conduct an investigation. It had been twenty-five years since Haines had done any sort of detective work, when he chased horse thieves in Labette County, Kansas. Haines had quickly accepted Shepherd's offer of five dollars per day plus expenses to watch the Connor, as catching gamblers was preferable to going after rustlers.

Haines registered at the hotel on a Saturday afternoon under the name of Jones, from Muskogee, Oklahoma, although it is unclear why he felt the need to use an alias. After checking into room 827, Haines decided to lie low for a day so as not to arouse unnecessary suspicion. The next evening, through a bellboy, he learned that something interesting was going on in room 802. Haines knocked on the door, was allowed in and saw someone operating a roulette wheel. He bought a dollar's worth of chips, lost them on the wheel and then made a beeline for Shepherd's office.

Shepherd quickly summoned Humes, who determined that the Connor must be raided immediately, before the evidence disappeared. Police sergeant William Gibson, lumber dealer Nathaniel Reeder Stanford and deputy marshal Sherman Fones accompanied the mayor to the hotel shortly before 9:00 p.m. There they split into two groups of two, meeting on the eighth floor. They entered room 802, which was unlocked, and noticed a roulette wheel sitting on a beautiful walnut table. Fred Firey, from the House of Lords raid the year before, was seated on a stool near the table, and a man named Walter Miller—the brother of Mose Miller, who ran the "gambling hell" at Fifth and Main—stood nearby.

Firey and Walter Miller, the only occupants of the room, were arrested, charged with gambling and released after posting $1,000 bond each. Humes confiscated the roulette wheel and the table, which measured eight feet long and four and a half feet wide, plus a poker table, poker chips and $218 in cash. The roulette wheel, valued at $800, likely was the same one Firey had been using at the House of Lords.

Humes issued a warrant for the arrest of F.W. Young, the manager of the Connor, for allowing a gambling device to be operated in the hotel. "I don't see how an article of furniture of that size could have been spirited into the hotel without someone being cognizant of it," the mayor told the *News Herald* the next morning.

Young, after posting a $500 bond, seemed indignant when questioned by the newspaper. "We don't make a personal inspection of all the baggage that is brought into the hotel," he said. "The baggage comes in through the alley and the guests come in through the front. When they register we don't ask them what they have in their baggage. We don't make a personal investigation of it. If they smuggle a roulette wheel into their room we are not responsible. I can say this, though, if we get the slightest hint that gambling is in progress, we will see to it that it is stopped."

In an editorial the afternoon after the raid, the *News Herald* suggested that Young may have known exactly what was occurring on his eighth floor and that a change in management would be welcome. "Without presuming to state who is 'back' of this gambling room, the fact remains that changed conditions would be welcomed by the people of Joplin at the Connor. The traveling men have not been making the right sort of reports regarding certain features of the present management. Driven out of the usual haunts, there is no reason why the monument to Tom Connor should be the refuge of the gambling fraternity."

The Connor heirs were dumbfounded at the accusations. "We do not lease the hotel for a gambling house," nephew Jerry O'Connor told a reporter. "I consider it an outrage. I am sure that Mr. Dean would never knowingly permit anything of that kind. This hotel was not put up to make money for the owners, and the lease is liberal enough to ensure the right kind of business."

Humes telephoned D.J. Dean in Kansas City and broke the news to him. He said no action would be taken until his brother, A.J., returned from a trip to New York but reassured the mayor that they were unaware that gambling had been occurring in the hotel. One of the Deans, on a recent visit to Joplin, said they had turned down an offer of $1,500 per month from a gambler to operate a game in the hotel.

Meanwhile, the hotel was getting a national black eye as such newspapers as the *Indianapolis Star*, the *Des Moines Register* and the *Salt Lake Tribune* ran wire service stories about the "fashionable million dollar Connor hotel" being raided for harboring gamblers. The *Webb City Register* jumped on as well, pointing out that the Connor "is getting a good deal of free advertising now but of rather an unfavorable kind."

Firey, Miller and Young all faced hearings in both city police court and state court. The city wasted little time in putting Young on trial. Just eight days after the raid, Young went on trial for permitting a gambling device to be maintained in the hotel. Perl Decker, who would go on to serve three terms in Congress; Shepherd; and a third attorney represented the city. When the trial began at 4:00 p.m., the courtroom was packed with ministers, city officials, Connor Hotel employees, lawyers, firemen, gamblers, "north end negroes" and other spectators.

The prosecution's witnesses included members of the raiding party, a chambermaid, a housekeeper and a former employee who had been fired by Young. The chambermaid testified that she had noticed the bed had been removed from room 802 about a week before the raid and that the roulette wheel and table were sitting in the hallway. The housekeeper's testimony was more devastating: she said Young had instructed her to remove the bed and had asked her if she had any canvas to cover the floor. In response to a question from the prosecution, she said it was not unusual for gambling devices to be taken into the hotel.

Robert Jacobin, who swept hallways and cleaned bathtubs at the Connor before his dismissal, testified that he had heard the whirling of a roulette wheel, the cries of "cash" and the clanking of roulette chips coming out of room 802. He said Young had approached him and asked, "So you are the boy who is going to make trouble about that wheel?" After the manager fired him, Jacobin threatened to expose the hotel. He did just that, going straight to the mayor with his story.

The defense called several other employees as witnesses, including the head porter, who said he was unaware of any gambling devices in the hotel. Three or four bellhops swore that there had never been any gambling in the building, they had never heard any strange sounds coming out of room 802, they had never seen anyone enter the room and Young had never even been on the eighth floor. "What is your duty at the hotel?" Decker asked one of them. "To answer calls, carry ice water, run errands, and—" at which point the city attorney interrupted him. "To keep your mouth shut?"

The trial continued on for more than ten hours, with only two five-minute recesses. This provided opportunity for the ministers who were present to examine the roulette wheel, which had been brought into the courtroom as evidence. The gamblers in attendance graciously explained how money was won and lost on the wheel.

Young finally took the stand as the last witness. He denied having the confrontation with Jacobin or having knowledge of any gambling devices in the hotel. As for the alleged removal of the bed in room 802, he said the housekeeper rather than the manager would have given the order. The prosecution did not cross-examine him. After lengthy closing arguments, the case went to the jury shortly before 2:00 a.m.

The six-member jury returned a verdict of not guilty less than fifteen minutes later. The courtroom was still packed, as the first all-night trial in Joplin's history captivated the audience. As expected, Joplin's ministerial community didn't care much for the "remarkable" outcome. "The verdict was a travesty of justice, an outrage on the decent citizenship of Joplin, in my opinion," Reverend C.M. Davenport of the Methodist Episcopal Church, South, told the *Joplin News Herald*. "I listened to the evidence from start to finish, and I cannot comprehend how six men could have acquitted the defendant. When evidence was brought out that Manager Young had told the housekeeper to move the beds from one room to another and secure a piece of canvas, if possible, to spread over the floor, it certainly looked conclusive that the manager had some idea for what purpose the apartment was to be used."

Reverend W.M. Cleaveland of the First Presbyterian Church didn't mince any words. "Whatever I might say in regard to the Young case and the decision wouldn't look well in print. Just put it down that what I think is too strong for printers' ink."

Young wasn't out of the woods entirely, however. He still faced the state case, which had been scheduled to begin less than eight hours after the jury's verdict. Young's attorney, William N. Andrews, opposed the quick turnaround. "I spent the greater part of last night fighting the case in the city court and don't feel in physical condition to try the case today," he told the judge. Humes opposed any delay, claiming that it would be of great inconvenience to the state's witnesses if they had to return at a later date for the trial. It ended up being another victory for the defense, as the judge postponed the trial one week.

The next day, in an editorial titled "The Shame of a City," the *Joplin Globe* acknowledged that a jury had found Young not guilty of committing a possible felony and that it would accept the jury's findings. "So, the public opinion of Joplin today will say that F.W. Young did not know that gambling was being conducted in the Connor hotel. BUT PUBLIC OPINION EMPHATICALLY HOLDS THAT F.W. YOUNG, AS MANAGER OF THE CONNOR HOTEL, OUGHT TO HAVE KNOWN THAT GAMBLING WAS BEING CONDUCTED IN THAT HOTEL," the newspaper shouted.

The state case against Young was not as contentious, although most of the players were the same. Much of the testimony in the three-hour trial was the same as before. The housekeeper told a slightly different story this time, claiming that someone—she did not specify who—had ordered her to remove the bed from room 802 around November 27.

The six-man jury included John F. Wise, president of the Miners Bank. Wise had pledged $2,000 to Tom Connor in 1906 for building the hotel, yet prosecuting attorney Byron Coon did not think to disqualify him. This jury, whose combined wealth was conservatively estimated at $500 million, deliberated only a single minute before returning a not guilty verdict.

Billy Sunday, who was still in Joplin leading a series of revivals, couldn't hide his disgust in his sermon the following evening. "I suppose they had that material up in the Connor just for an ornament to the room; they had the rugs placed on the floor to kneel on and were holding prayer meetings in that room. Any fool can understand that they did not have that roulette wheel up there to gamble on. They just had it there because it was a beautiful piece of furniture."

The evangelist ended his six weeks in Joplin with a final sermon on Sunday evening, January 2, 1910. According to the *Joplin Globe*, Sunday drew a total crowd of 273,000 in Joplin, with an average evening attendance of 6,000.

This roulette wheel, on display at the Joplin Museum Complex, may be the one used by gambler Fred Firey. *Joplin Historical and Mineral Museum.*

He collected $5,286 during his final day in the city and used that amount to pay himself and his staff and to cover expenses.

Acting city attorney Perl Decker tried four times to have Walter Miller and Fred Firey convicted of setting up and operating a gambling device in the Connor Hotel. The first trial resulted in a hung jury, and seven weeks later, another jury couldn't make up its mind either but voted five to one in favor of acquittal. The third trial resulted in another hung jury, three to three. Finally, the fourth trial settled the matter once and for all: the prosecution could not prove that the two were in charge of the room, had set up the roulette wheel or were engaged in gambling. The jury was out only a few minutes before returning a not guilty verdict.

The only remaining mystery was the roulette wheel itself. If Miller and Firey did not bring it to the eighth floor of the Connor, then who did? In all likelihood, it belonged to Firey, who had been seen operating a roulette wheel—perhaps the same one—at the House of Lords a year and a half before. The Connor Hotel wheel would remain as police property until the rightful owner claimed it and faced the legal consequences.

On display at the Joplin Museum Complex is a roulette wheel, donated by Rolla Stephens and Verne Wilder, said to be from the House of Lords. It's entirely possible that this is the infamous Fred Firey wheel.

NEW MANAGEMENT

Although the Dean brothers had claimed that the Connor was losing money, the *Globe* reported in February 1910 that the hotel was making a "neat profit." It is likely that the proprietors had not fully recovered the $115,000 investment in furnishings in only two years of operation. Still, the Deans had grown weary of overseeing their Joplin property and preferred to concentrate their efforts on the magnificent Hotel Baltimore in Kansas City. Quietly, they began looking for someone to purchase their lease on the building.

The Deans had to look no further than their own Hotel Baltimore to find someone with the financial means to buy out their stock in the Connor Hotel Company. Colonel Willis Wood, who had made a fortune selling dry goods and manufacturing clothing in St. Joseph, Missouri, had moved to Kansas City around the turn of the century and settled in at the Baltimore.

To manage the Connor and become his partner, the English-born Wood turned to Theodore B. (T.B.) Baker, who had just sold the one-hundred-room Goodlander Hotel at Fort Scott, Kansas. The deal closed on June 2, 1910, for "well above $100,000," which included the building lease and hotel furnishings.

"We intend to improve every department, and will spare no expense to make the Connor equal in every respect to the best hotels in America," Baker told the *Globe*. "The appointments are more expensive, in many respects, than those in some of the most pretentious eastern hotels. I have in mind a number of improvements by which I hope to increase the patronage of Joplin people. No detail of the service, cuisine or equipment will be overlooked."

It was Baker's belief that the hotel's service did not measure up to its grandeur. He convinced French chef Jacques Jaquin to come from New York. For the next three years, Monsieur Jaquin would dazzle Connor patrons with his magnificent creations. Baker even sent him on a three-week tour of St. Louis, Chicago, Philadelphia and New York in 1913 to visit with the country's best chefs and bring back ideas for the hotel's dining rooms and Roof Garden.

Joplin's coming-out party as a major convention city occurred in 1912. The city hosted the Democratic State Convention (1,200 delegates), the Missouri Bankers Association (900 attendees), the United Commercial Travelers (1,500 delegates and wives), the Central States Exhibitors' Association (175 to 200 guests) and the National Association of Sanitary Engineers (300 guests). Despite having the Connor, which could accommodate 350, the city faced an acute hotel shortage. Every boarding and rooming house available was pressed into service, as well as several private residences. Dozens of the bankers had to stay in the sleeping cars that brought them to Joplin. Those coming from St. Joseph lodged at the "Hotel Missouri Pacific," the St. Louisans and Kansas Citians resided at the "Hotel Frisco" and others from Kansas City stayed at the "Hotel Southern."

Aside from the conventions, the most exciting news of 1912 in Joplin was the formal opening of the Connor Roof Garden on August 7. The Dieter & Wenzel Construction Company had left an unfinished Roof Garden four years earlier, and Baker decided to make some modifications and open it to the public. He explained, "Modern tendencies are strongly toward outdoor life, and we are trying to do our part. We are hoping that people who seek a cool, pleasant place to eat or buy a cold drink in the evening will get in the habit of coming to our Roof Garden. There will always be plenty of fresh air, and nothing is more healthful."

Baker added a kitchen on the roof and tables to accommodate 150 people, placed strings of colored lightbulbs all around, constructed a fish pond with a fountain in the middle and built a stage for the hotel's orchestra. Professor Victor G. Kreyer was in charge of the eight-piece orchestra, accompanied by two soloists. The entire space was decorated with palms, ferns, flowers and Japanese lanterns, but it was the goslings and one hundred goldfish swimming among the rocks of the mining district that drew the most attention on opening night.

Baker couldn't have been more pleased with the turnout. The *News Herald* reported a crowd of 1,000, while the *Globe* used the manager's estimate of 1,500 based on the number of elevator trips made throughout the evening. Baker had arranged for a special "to the Roof Garden only" elevator that could carry 10 people to the top in ninety seconds, but at times it was necessary to utilize the hotel's second elevator to help ferry passengers up and down. Every woman in attendance received a "handsome" fan, and punch and cake were served to everyone.

Four days after the grand opening, the *Joplin Morning Tribune* suggested that Baker might want to use the space for another purpose: "He has ample space for a tennis court up in the ozone there and by clearing the tables in the afternoon he could offer this as an inducement to the enthusiasts in the afternoon. We hardly believe the roof is large enough for a football field."

But Baker had no plans for a tennis court. The Roof Garden would be much more valuable for other purposes.

SOFT EVENING BREEZES
NINE STORIES UP

Few nightspots or entertainment venues in Joplin's history have captivated the public the way the Connor Hotel's Roof Garden did during the second decade of the twentieth century. "Atop the Connor" was the place to be seen while enjoying the evening breezes and first-rate entertainment nine stories above the ground. Perhaps the novelty of being higher than anyone else in the four-state area contributed to the appeal; at any rate, people flocked to the rooftop from Joplin and neighboring cities alike.

Rooftop gardens were becoming the rage everywhere. According to Theodore Osmundson in his *Roof Gardens: History, Design, and Construction*, hotels and restaurants in New York adopted the trend from theaters and proceeded to outdo them. "The roof garden atop the Hotel Astor was one of the most outstanding of its time, from the early 1920s to just after World War II," he wrote. The concept spread onto the roofs of expensive new apartments bordering Central Park, and penthouses with roof gardens became status symbols for those who could afford them.

In Joplin, the five-story Olivia Apartments at Fourth and Moffet, five blocks west of the Connor, had a roof garden that offered a view of Webb City on clear days. The six-story Newman Mercantile Company, completed in 1910, opened a roof garden for its employees in April 1914. It included a dancing pavilion, lawn swings, flowers boxes and a piano. A special feature was a lunchroom, where its 150 employees could eat "far above the noise and bustle of the busy rooms beneath, their faces cooled by a breeze that moves unfettered above hot pavements."

The Newman family permitted an employee Newman Social Club, which elected its own officers, to manage the roof garden. An entertainment committee of the club scheduled the musical entertainment and dances. The store provided a reception for its employees on Thursday evenings, and occasionally they were allowed to bring their friends.

When the Junge Baking Company built a new $100,000 plant at Eighteenth and Main in 1915 to produce its Tip-Top Bread, it included a roof garden. Intended as a "playground" for its employees, the roof garden also featured a bandstand for the thirty-five-piece Junge employee band to practice and perform. J.B. Kreyer, brother of the Connor Hotel orchestra leader, directed the band.

Connor manager T.B. Baker, who would go on to become a successful hotel owner and developer in Texas, realized that a popular roof garden would further distinguish the Connor and add to its luster. He also wanted something that could compete with Lakeside Park, the popular attraction built by Alfred H. Rogers on Center Creek between Joplin and Carthage.

Rogers opened Lakeside Park in 1895 as a destination for his Southwest Missouri Electric Railway. Admission to the trolley park was free, as long as visitors paid twenty-five cents for a round-trip ticket from Joplin. Lakeside featured swimming, boating, picnicking, a swinging bridge, baseball games, a roller coaster, fireworks, silent movies, a dance pavilion and Sunday band concerts.

Baker hoped that he could siphon off some of the Lakeside crowds attracted to the parties, free concerts and nightly dancing in the pavilion by offering these activities without the long trolley rides. He hired the best publicity man in Joplin, Sol (Solomon) Dan, away from Electric Park and the Empress Theatre to manage his Roof Garden.

Born in Taurage, Lithuania (then part of the Russian empire), in 1882, Sol Dan and his family emigrated from eastern Europe to Memphis. Dan had the gift of gab and delighted acquaintances with his tall tales. He worked as a newspaper reporter in Nashville, was press agent for the Shubert Theatre in Birmingham, Alabama, and the Bijou Theatre in Memphis and even managed a one-man play called *The Mysterious Mr. Skylark Holmes* in Nashville before arriving in Joplin in 1912. That summer, he managed to secure a thirty-five-member comic opera company from Hot Springs, Arkansas, to perform for ten weeks at Electric Park in Schifferdecker Park.

When Baker announced his hiring in February 1913, Dan outlined his lofty goals for the Roof Garden. "I intend to give the people of Joplin, those who are lovers of things Bohemian and of the gay lights, the realistic," he told the *Joplin Morning Tribune*. "Their dreams will come true, as the Connor hotel Roof Garden will be equipped in the best style and will be made the best garden in the west. This is a broad statement, but it is true. Joplin is admirably situated for a Roof Garden and the location of the Connor hotel is very good. Here the soft evening breezes may blow away the cares of the hot summer days and on the roof everything will be cool and nice."

Dan promised cabaret entertainers, vaudeville, a symphony orchestra and a Hungarian band, but he drew the line at acrobatic or dog acts. Baker came up with a system where patrons could call the hotel and reserve a table for any evening. He also had the Roof Garden remodeled to include an electric kitchen, pantry and service stands so that a waitstaff of twenty-four could provide café service and refreshments with minimal wait times.

Three elevators ferried passengers nine floors up. The open-air space had a seating capacity of six hundred, which included booths for private parties along the walls and numerous tables in the center. There was no admission charge; Dan liked to say that a man with only ten cents was as welcome as a man with $1 million.

A marketing whiz ahead of his time, Dan coined the catchphrase "Atop the Connor," which would serve the hotel long after he departed Joplin. He also initiated the Cabaret Revue, featuring vaudeville acts and a twenty-piece orchestra directed by Victor Kreyer.

The Cabaret Revue and remodeled Roof Garden made their formal debut on Friday evening, May 30, 1913. According to the *Joplin News Herald*, "Hundreds of society folk from Joplin, Webb City and Carthage" enjoyed the performers and decorations consisting of plants and varicolored lights. The elevators were in constant use, as it was standing room only on the roof until eleven o'clock.

Both Joplin newspapers continued to wax enthusiastically about the nightspot. (Joplin was now a two-newspaper town, as the *Morning Tribune* had gone out of business on April 11.) The *News Herald* reported, "The roof is the most pleasant spot in all Joplin, there being absolutely nothing to bar the way of the breezes, and with a café service such as is offered by Manager Baker a delightful evening can be had at this popular amusement place." The *Globe* chimed in: "It seems as though Joplin has gone Cabaret wild and that the Connor roof will serve capacity audiences goes without saying."

The Cabaret Revue advertised being open every night from 7:30 p.m. to midnight, although crowds seldom stayed quite that long. If visitors from Carthage and Galena, Kansas, didn't catch the last streetcar at 10:55 p.m., it was more expensive to take a taxi or touring car home. Fortunately, the Myers Taxicab Company had its headquarters right in the Connor Hotel, and patrons had only to dial "21" to summon one.

Dan added a ragtime performer and hit on the idea of staging an "Oriental Festival" featuring such delicacies as chop suey, yet-ca-mein soup, steamed rice, oolong tea and Chinese desserts. Special menus were prepared and the roof was decorated in yellow and red bunting and Chinese lanterns, but the opening had to be delayed a week when "chill weather" unexpectedly hit Joplin.

Joplinites celebrated the Fourth of July atop the Connor with a patriotic song revue and ice cream festival in the afternoon and eight cabaret performers from 6:00 p.m. to 12:30 a.m. "Within the sight of fireworks that flared for miles around, a large throng spent the evening of the Fourth on the Connor hotel Roof Garden, far removed from the noise and stress of the celebration on the streets," reported the *Globe*. "A cool, brisk gale was wafted across the roof and the gladsome song of cabaret singers mingled with the talk and laughter about the festal board."

Dan continued to come up with innovative ways to entice new and old customers alike to take the elevators nine floors up. He encouraged patrons to bring their children for a "Kid Kabaret" from 6:00 p.m. to 8:30 p.m. "This will give the children plenty of time to get to bed early, where they can dream of all the fine things they saw on the Roof Garden," read an advertorial in the *News Herald*. Dan also scheduled an amateur night, a request night, a "Festival of Ni-L-Poj" (Joplin spelled backward), a Texas Tommy dance night and a special menu night.

The food served on the roof turned out to be nearly as big a draw as the entertainment. Patrons had an enormous variety of items to choose from, including fixed-price table d'hôte French and Italian meals. The 1913 menu included the following à la carte items:

- *Lobster or crabmeat cocktail, 40 cents*
- *Caviar on toast, 50 cents*
- *Sardines on toast, 35 cents*
- *Anchovy on toast, 40 cents*
- *Lake Superior trout, 50 cents*
- *Spanish mackerel, 50 cents*

- *Halibut, 50 cents*
- *Soft-shell crab, 55 cents*
- *Filet of sole, 45 cents*
- *Frogs (fried, plain, or breaded), 55 cents*
- *Lobster Newburg, 75 cents or $1.25 for two*
- *Lobster American, 75 cents or $1.25 for two*
- *Lobster New Orl'ns, 75 cents or $1.25 for two*
- *Crabmeat Newburg, 75 cents or $1.25 for two*
- *Crabmeat Fedora, 85 cents or $1.50 for two*
- *Crabmeat Dewey, 85 cents or $1.50 for two*

Given his journalistic background, it shouldn't have been a big surprise when Dan announced that the Connor would become the first hotel in the United States to publish its own newspaper. *Atop the Connor Bulletin* made its debut on Sunday, July 27, 1913, with the explanation that it would be published occasionally "for the sole purpose of creating interest in higher class entertainment and for the singing of praises of the Cool Connor Roof."

The eight-page paper boasted an impressive number of ads from such Joplin mainstays as Rosenberg's Shoe Store, Newman's, Ramsay's, Union Oyster Company, Miners Bank, Joplin National Bank, Jackson Drug Company and Empire District Electric Company. The popular beers served on the roof—Falstaff, Pabst Blue Ribbon, Anheuser-Busch and Schlitz—each purchased a quarter-page ad. Other beverages available on the roof—Waterfill & Frazier whiskey, Nicholson's 1843 Whiskey, Welch's Grape Juice and Coca-Cola—were also featured in ads.

Never one to stay long in any particular place, Dan left Joplin in the fall of 1913. He would go on to work for the Fort Smith (Arkansas) Furniture Company, operate the Wichita Falls (Texas) Opera Company, serve as business manager of the *Fayetteville (AR) Daily Leader* and run an advertising agency. For several years, he was an automobile show promoter in Tulsa.

Baker, who had managed the Connor since June 1910, made a startling announcement via telegram in March 1914: he had signed a ten-year lease to manage the St. Anthony Hotel in San Antonio. Built by two cattlemen in 1909, the ten-story, 450-room hotel was the first luxury hotel in San Antonio.

Baker named his older brother, W.R. (William Rodem) Baker, who had joined the Connor staff several months earlier, resident manager of the Joplin hotel. He sent Carl Hammond, the assistant manager of the Connor and his longtime right-hand man, to be the assistant manager of the St.

ATOP THE
CONNOR BULLETIN

Volume I	Joplin, Mo., Week of July 27, 1913	Number 1.

CONNOR CABARET VERITABLE TRIUMPH

Thousands of Enthusiastic Patrons Enjoy Unique Entertainment Amid Cooling Breezes

REAL STARS PRESENTED

Many People Journey From Neighboring Cities to Attend the Show Atop the Popular Hotel.

Amid the hearty and appreciative applause of over three thousand people, the Connor Cabaret was opened on the evening of May 30th, and nightly since there has been atop this popular hostelry a merry throng, who have attended the festivities and have declared this unique entertainment to be superior to any presentation ever offered in the entire Southwest.

The performance is a varied one, ranging from character impersonations to classical vocal selections, and each number is received with a spontaneous yea of approval. Vaudeville stars who have heretofore appeared only in the larger theatres of the East and West are being featured on the Roof, and as each has won additional honors here. The Roof this year has been entirely remodeled. Two new

buildings now house a modern and sanitary kitchen, with the latest electrical ranges, and a service pantry, commodious and from where the daintiest of edibles are being served. Booths for private dinner parties have been arranged along the walls, while in the center of the garden, tables have been placed so as to permit dining while viewing the Cabaret. Flowers, vines and plants have been artistically arranged, and altogether no prettier, cooler or more inviting amusement place can be found, all this great, too free.

During the few past weeks there have been seen "atop the Connor" such artists as Ralph Snyder, Harry Belding, Myrtle Souders, Esther Johnson, Nell Scott, Ward Perry, Ned LaRose, Grace Perry and many other artists of exceptional ability.

ARTIST SALARIES
COSTLY TO CONNOR.

Be it understood that Joplin is now in the first rank of cities presenting Cabaret performances. Artists' salaries have become a secondary consideration with the management, and this season will find a number of acts never before appearing off the vaudeville stage. This applies to Santucci, Libernati and several other celebrities who will be brought to this city for an early showing.

Greeters in Old Arkansas.

(Special to the Bulletin)
Fort Smith, Ark., July 26, 1913.—Three well-known Greeters are found at the hotels in Fort Smith, Ark., and they have done much to make that place a popular tourist resort. Pleasant J. Davis, who is secretary of the Arkansas Greeters' Association, is chief clerk of the Hotel Main. His first name is appropriate, as his jovial smile is always present as he greets his guests. He is better known to his friends as "Jack." Edward V. Fetty, a member of the board of governors of the Greeters, is night clerk at the Hotel Main. Mr. Fetty has the happy faculty of making his guests feel at home, even before they have signed their name to the register. W. U. Malone, president of the Arkansas Greeters, and until recently chief clerk of the Goldman Hotel but now its manager, is another of those prince of good fellows who help to place the hotel on the high plane.

The Connor Cabaret now presents an orchestra composed of the best soloists hereabouts. The organization is under the direction of Prof. Vic Kreyer and each evening an excellent program of popular and classical selections is rendered.

MANY INNOVATIONS
PLANNED FOR ROOF.

Manager Baker is contemplating a number of innovations on the Roof, and ere the summer season has waned, patrons will find many new features to amuse and delight them during the hot months. The Connor's popular manager is pleased with the way Joplinites have greeted his latest venture and declares that nothing is too good for his patrons. While his plans are but in the making, he positively says that he is a staunch Missourian and will show them.

Clever Artist Booked Here.

Manager Sol Dan of the Connor Roof Garden declares that he will uncork a real novelty entertainer shortly by presenting Chicago's favorite artist, Cora Fredericks. This charming comedienne has appeared in the leading Cabarets of the East and West, and was for more than eight months the principal feature at the Wintergarten, San Francisco. Miss Fredericks is scheduled to begin her engagement "Atop the Connor" the week of July 27.

Connor Roof Enforces Rule.

Manager Baker of the Connor Hotel Company has posted cards about the Roof calling attention to the fact that the Garden is private property and that the management reserves the right to refuse admission to all persons deemed objectionable. This rule is being strictly enforced, with the result that patrons of the Roof Garden are confident of its refined environment.

The people of Webb City talk enthusiastically of the merits of the Roof Garden and assist in the merry-making at this popular and cool resort.

CONNOR MANAGER

T. B. BAKER

Joplin is fortunate in having secured such a man as T. B. Baker. Endowed with natural talent for serving the public, he came to Joplin two years ago and took charge of the Connor Hotel. Upon the day he arrived here he threw his lot into the business spirit. From the day the Connor Hotel, T. B. Baker, and boosting have been synonymous in public enterprise of merit is called to receive the support of this popular hotel manager. When the improvement was inaugurated to take such steps to carry forward that organization. When the Provident Association wanted a place to hold its annual charity ball, he came forward and offered the use of the hotel. When the Noonday Luncheon Club was founded of some of the best business men in Joplin, naturally its turned to the Connor and its meetings have been held there ever since.

When the Civic Club was founded, the Connor was the natural location. Other local organizations have taken advantage of his hospitality until the Connor is now regarded as the meeting place for committees, clubs and other organizations of public character.

Last Summer when Mr. Baker determined to give Joplin a touch of high life by opening the Roof Garden, it was not done for what he could get out of it, but for the advertisement the city would receive. This year the enlarged Roof Garden has served even more as an advertisement for the community and rich and poor, young and old, gather there in the evenings to enjoy the cool breezes that can always be found at such an altitude.

To Mr. Baker's ingenuity, farsightedness and public spirit and hard work can be attributed the success of this big institution, and, as one of his friends put it, "Baker has made the Connor more than a hotel—he has made it a public institution."

OUT-OF-TOWN FOLKS
VISIT THE ROOF

The Cabaret was much enjoyed one night last week by Mr. and Mrs. Chandler of Seneca, Mo., who were the guests of Miss Edith Ferguson. The party was highly pleased with the entertainment "atop" and said a very pleasant evening was the result of their visit.

Shriners at The Cabaret.

The Shriners met in a business meeting "Atop the Connor" last week and, after setting things aright "along the desert," paid the Cabaret a visit in a body and were entertained by the artists. Every member voted the evening a most pleasant one and, besides saying many nice things of the place, assured the management they would return for more "Cabareting."

NEW YORK ENJOYS SUMMER GARDEN

The Terrace, a Most Inviting and Popular Recreation Place Open for the Summer Months.

SYMPHONY ORCHESTRA INSTALLED

Decorations and Illuminations Are Most Superb—Great Crowds Attend the Metropolis' Latest Cafe-Theatre.

(Special to the Bulletin)
New York, July 26, 1913.—Terrace Garden, between Fifty-eighth and Fifty-ninth streets near Lexington avenue, has long been one of the favored dining, wining and joy-making places of New Yorkers. For a long course of years it has maintained and added to its prestige, in the face of an ever growing number of new establishments. This is due principally to the good judgment of its management and the attractive character of the Garden itself.

During the Summer months the open-air garden attracts many, many visitors. On any evening upon which one may chance to drop into this delightful retreat there is certain to be found a numerous crowd, and a happy one. There is something about the place that warms the cockles of the coldest hearts. It may be the delicacies of the menu, the wine, the sense of good fellowship evidenced by the surrounding crowds, or the harmony of a dreamy air rendered by the well-selected orchestra. Probably all of these influences enter into this very desirable result, but certain is it that the casual visitor of a hot Summer night departs feeling younger and kinder to his fellows.

The garden is decorated in a way that is just a bit different from most similar places. True, there are the usual palms, plants and flowers, with the customary colored electric bulbs and the other time-honored paraphernalia of a Summer Garden. They are much the same, certainly, but there is an individuality about their arrangement, an indefinable something that makes the whole ensemble refreshingly new. This atmosphere is enhanced by the quiet courtesy of attendants and the excellent direction of details that eliminates jarring, material things. To visit Terrace Garden when the mind is tired and the spirit low is to find a quiet relaxation which produces a new reason for going on and a greater willingness for the going.

CABARET STARS
TO APPEAR HERE.

The List Includes a Hungarian Orchestra and Other Features.

During the summer season "Atop the Connor" there will appear a galaxy of stars seldom seen in the Southwest. These engagements have been made possible only through arrangements with the agencies of the East and by the payment of salaries said to exceed those paid vaudeville stars playing the larger cities. Among the entertainers to appear here will be musical specialties, operatic duos, comedy quartettes, a Hungarian orchestra and chic soubrettes. The best talent obtainable from Ragtime Land will be seen here, and there will never be a week pass but what a substantial list of clever and versatile artists will appear at this cool amusement resort. The programme nightly begins at 7:30 and continues through until midnight.

The Connor became the first hotel in the United States to publish its own newspaper. Joplin
Historical & Mineral Museum.

Anthony. Baker said he would split his own time between the two hotels. "While the St. Anthony is one of the best hotels in the South, and while I shall be glad to have it under my control, I do not want my friends in this part of the country to feel that I am going to leave here," he explained. "There are no better people on earth than those with whom I have come into touch in Joplin, and I hope to be able to continue to be one of them."

W.R. Baker decided to focus on improving the food, drink and service on his rooftop. He moved the kitchen, supply room and serving area closer to the action, hired additional waiters and decorated the space with flowers, vines, Japanese lanterns and lights of various colors. There were enough tables to accommodate 350 people. Baker also hired Kreyer and his six-piece orchestra to provide music for the cabaret performers he had booked.

The resident manager advertised the Roof Garden as "the coolest place to be found within 300 miles of Joplin" and "the coolest place in the Southwest." An estimated six hundred people attended the opening of the 1914 season on June 18. Because of the size of the crowd, W.R. Baker had two performances occurring simultaneously—one on the east side and another on the west side of the roof.

It should be no surprise that other ideas emerged for use of the rooftop. Hugh Robinson, a famous aviator from Neosho, proposed a biplane service between Joplin and Neosho that would turn the Connor roof into an aerodrome. Robinson, who was the first person to use an aircraft for emergency assistance, on Lake Michigan in 1911, claimed that he could make the twenty-mile trip between the two cities in thirty minutes while carrying two passengers. He went so far as to order a plane from the Wright brothers' factory in Dayton, Ohio, but apparently never consulted the Baker brothers, who likely wouldn't have been willing to relinquish the roof for such purposes.

A Connor manager in 1919, however, said that a landing field and hangar on the hotel roof wasn't such a bad idea. As the city of Joplin began exploring the creation of a landing field to take advantage of planned air routes throughout the country, John W. Howell said it didn't take "an improbable stretch of imagination" to put it on the rooftop. Ultimately, a private landing field at Seventh Street and Schifferdecker Avenue was established several years before the city built a municipal airport.

Prior to the 1915 rooftop season, the Connor estate announced that it had extended the lease to the Baker brothers for another ten years. W.R. Baker took the opportunity to reveal that they would spend $10,000 to build a new convention hall for Joplin on the east side of the roof so the hotel could host state conventions and parties. He replaced Kreyer's orchestra with a five-piece Mexican ensemble and hired four cabaret singers and two dancers. He placed ads in the *Tulsa World* and other newspapers to promote opening night, June 16. His efforts paid off when an estimated one thousand people streamed in.

Even a cabaret tax of three dollars per day, or eighty dollars per month, passed by the Joplin city commission later that month didn't slow the Connor's momentum. The tax applied only to the hotel, as it operated the city's lone cabaret.

Despite not charging any admission, the Connor still managed to attract some of the nation's top cabaret and character singers. Baker brought in the Senate Four, from New York; Beulah Baer, from New York and Chicago; and Victor Fredrick, from Chicago. Two Kansas newspapers seventy miles away both reported that the "Roof Garden is a right busy place on Saturday nights." Unfortunately, continued rains cut the 1915 season short by a week.

Inclement weather would not be a problem the next year, as the Connor opened a six-hundred-seat convention hall on the east wing of the roof in May. The oval-shaped, steel structure with reinforced concrete opened on May 4 with a Shrine Club dinner-dance. The Connor also installed a canopy over the entire garden space. "While we do not anticipate such a rainy season as annoyed us last year, we are prepared," explained William Hanner, the hotel's chief clerk.

The hotel advertised the fact that it had spent $25,000 on remodeling the roof, which included the open-air section and the enclosed auditorium. Both spaces could be used for the cabarets, depending on the weather

Left: The Connor opened an enclosed Roof Garden in 1916. *Joplin Historical & Mineral Museum.*

Opposite: The enclosed Roof Garden is visible in this 1919 photo. *Joplin Historical & Mineral Museum.*

and the size of the crowds. More than one thousand turned out for the opening night of the 1916 season, enjoying the seven performers and the five-piece orchestra.

W.R. Baker, eager to meet his brother's expectations, pulled out all the stops to recoup the money. He advertised Sunday dinners, complete with "nice, clean entertainers." He brought in an orchestra composed of eight native Hawaiians to increase interest in the hotel's evening dinner dances. He secured a French-English ballet dancer named M'lle. Tatziva, whose barefoot interpretive dancing (such as to the God of Wine and Plenty) packed the rooftop. And to close the season, he presented "A Night in Dixie" featuring an African American orchestra and quartet, buck-and-wing dancing and a cakewalk.

The convention hall/auditorium became known as the Winter Garden in the fall of 1916. Rather than using the rooftop only during the summer, the Connor management could book conventions and special activities throughout the year. A cabaret dinner dance on Halloween and a firemen's benefit ball on Thanksgiving night paled in comparison to the New Year's "greeting party," which began at 10:30 p.m. on the evening of January 1. The *Globe* reporter who had the good fortune of covering the event no doubt enjoyed the experience:

> *It was the biggest Monday night celebration of the coming of a new year in the history of Joplin. Every table at the Connor was in use, the excellence of the service and the reputation of the Connor parties having attracted not only Joplin men and women but many from as far as 200 miles. At the House of Lords the S.R.O. (Standing Room Only) sign was still out at 1:20 o'clock this morning and a score of persons were waiting for an opportunity to obtain seats. At the Connor, the closing law went unrecognized long after 1 o'clock, a welcome, one-night-a-year from officials. Wine flowed freely.*

The New Year's party turned out to be the last hurrah for W.R. Baker, who announced in late January 1917 that he would be leaving for San Antonio to manage the St. Anthony and his brother's newest acquisition: the historic Menger Hotel. Located just a few steps from the Alamo, the 250-room Menger was widely known for its famous bar, where it is said that Theodore Roosevelt recruited his Rough Riders cavalry brigade in 1898.

The Bakers had a falling out, however, and W.R. never worked for his brother again. To replace his brother in Joplin, T.B. named John W. Howell, the Connor's general auditor, as resident manager. Howell had once taken a government auditor's exam in Washington, D.C., and placed fourth out of several hundred. He had experience as a bookkeeper and cashier before accepting a position with Baker as general auditor of St. Anthony Hotel in San Antonio.

Howell may have had the ability to balance a ledger, but he had little interest in bringing entertainment to the Roof Garden. Perhaps the novelty of the rooftop had worn off, but in any event, he scheduled only one major event during the summer of 1917: a troupe of five Spanish musicians and four singers and dancers for opening night on June 4. But in fairness to

Howell, the United States had declared war on Germany two months earlier and Joplinites were in little mood to go cabaret wild.

The Connor roof did host a farewell dinner and dance on September 19 for the 133 drafted men who made up Joplin's first quota for the U.S. National Army. The Independent Order of Odd Fellows band led a parade of the soldiers from Twelfth and Main to the hotel, as a crowd of more than 1,000 packed both sides of Main Street. A local committee raised more than $400 for the banquet, and the Connor provided the meal at a reduced rate and donated the $25 that its orchestra charged. The dinner was for the enlisted men only, but more than 100 women, friends and relatives joined them for the dance, which lasted past midnight. The men departed for Camp Funston at Fort Riley, Kansas, at 5:00 a.m. the next day, some of them never to return to their hometown.

Although he didn't have the flair of a Sol Dan or even a W.B. Baker, Howell did come up with the most unusual event ever seen on the Connor roof. For the hotel's annual Halloween party, he had a red barn built on the north wing of the Winter Garden and brought in at least one horse, cow, donkey, turkey and opossum, plus several chickens, ducks and geese from farms in the area. (It must have been quite a scene getting the critters on the elevator.) The decorations consisted of a rail fence, shocks of corn, autumn leaves, jack-o'-lanterns and silhouettes of witches, black cats and ghosts.

Three hundred invited guests paid two dollars each to attend the barnyard dinner and dance, with music provided by the Manuel Torres Spanish Orchestra. The *Joplin Globe* dutifully reported on the event the next day:

> The stoical cow and the patient donkey feasted on the edible part of the decorations, which tender-hearted dancers brought from the corners of the winter garden to their pens. Early in the evening Brer Possum escaped from his keeper and assumed a position in the extreme top of an autumn tree. He remained there throughout the evening, successfully resisting a hundred attempts to shake him from his post.
>
> Except when they were provoked by admiring fun-seekers, the ducks and geese maintained a dignified silence. When disturbed they squawked and clattered admirably, giving the affair the promised touch of rusticity.

On the morning of the Halloween party, Howell pledged that the hotel would participate in "Meatless Tuesdays" and "Wheatless Wednesdays," introduced by Herbert Hoover and the U.S. Food Administration as part of its "Food Will Win the War" campaign. Chicken, fish, seafood and lobster would be served in place of pork, beef and mutton on Tuesdays. Bread would be made of rye flour, barley, cornmeal and other grains on Wednesdays, and ice cream and fruit would be substituted for pastry desserts.

December 25 fell on a Tuesday, so the Connor's 1917 Christmas dinner, served from 11:30 a.m. to 9:00 p.m. for $1.50, had to be "meatless." Guests had a choice of three entrées: roast turkey with cranberry sauce, Watertown goose with apple compote or one-half grilled spring chicken on toast. The meal included fresh lobster cocktail, chicken gumbo or cream of tomato soup, salad, Brussels sprouts, mashed potatoes, ice cream and assorted cakes.

The Connor had a New Year's Eve watch party—which included flowers for the women, cigars for the men and souvenirs for all—but it didn't generate much excitement due to the war. In fact, the hotel's liquor sales were between one-half and two-thirds of the amount sold at the party the year before. The House of Lords saw its liquor consumption cut in half. A saloon man explained the situation to the *Globe*: "The people are just too serious to put on any big parties. Why, we came very near [to] not having any celebration at all. It was considered inadvisable for a time."

The hotel and its Roof Garden continued to figure prominently in the social life of Joplin in 1918, and as expected, most of the events had a war theme. An audience of five hundred at a YMCA father-and-son banquet on February 11 heard a Canadian lieutenant on leave discuss trench warfare and explain that the Allies were going to defeat the Huns because "North America has sent a type of men to the front that are not known there. They have more pep and vim than other soldiers and are largely responsible for what successes have been obtained. When the Americans get 'over there,' the Germans are going to get the worst licking of their lives."

The Joplin Business Women's Patriotic Society, formed at the request of the Red Cross, held a benefit dance at the hotel on April 24. Department store saleswomen were put in charge of the war relief effort, selling tickets for one dollar each. The event was supposed to be confined to the Winter Garden, but when so many tickets were bought they had to request that Howell open the entire hotel for the dancers. He wouldn't let them use the main dining room until 10:00 p.m., but by 9:00 p.m. the elevators to the roof had been shut down because that space was already at full capacity. The dancers commandeered the lobby, moving the big leather chairs and benches out of the way. "The guests literally danced all over the hotel," the *News Herald* reported. Given that more than $1,800 was raised, it can be assumed that at least 1,800 jammed the Connor that evening.

The Roof Garden hosted a "so long feast" on July 22 for those recently drafted into the U.S. National Army. These farewell banquets were becoming fairly commonplace, and most were held at the House of Lords. But this group contained 310 men—the largest contingent Joplin had ever sent to Camp Funston—and only the Connor had the space to accommodate them. Local citizens and companies contributed money on a weekly basis to a soldier banquet fund, but Selective Service was calling so many men from the Joplin district that the fund was often depleted.

Ten years after it opened, the Connor was firmly entrenched as the heart and soul of Joplin. A letter received by the general agent of Joplin's Frisco Station from a twenty-two-year-old Joplin soldier stationed in France is indicative of the affection the city had for its hotel. Paul Carey, serving with an ammunition train of the Thirty-Fifth Infantry Division, wrote in late June that the troops had seen some remarkable sights and camped near some historic places, "but the grandest sight of all right now to me would be the old Connor hotel on Fourth and Main streets, Joplin, Jasper county, Missouri."

As could be expected, many Joplinites celebrated the end of the Great War at the Connor Hotel and directly outside at Fourth and Main. The State Department announced the armistice at 1:45 a.m. Joplin time on Monday, November 11, and word reached the *News Herald* just a few minutes later. The newspaper notified the city's firemen, who raised residents from their slumber by blowing steam whistles. "Immediately men, women and children began pouring from all directions into the business section of the city and shortly after 3 o'clock there was a band of music, and by 4 o'clock three bands were playing," the paper reported.

Joplin mayor Jesse Osborne issued a proclamation at 3:45 a.m. declaring Monday, November 11, as a holiday and urging all business to be suspended. Shortly after, an impromptu parade consisting of the bands, pedestrians and automobiles started at Fourth and Main. "Thousands of people left their beds and ran to join the celebrators without taking time to fully dress themselves," the *News Herald* added. "Women in house dresses and long wraps; men without collars and ties, and a few in bathrobes were in the crowd."

In the Connor lobby, a band began playing "There'll Be a Hot Time in the Old Town Tonight" at 3:30 a.m. as people two-stepped to the music. "Partners were chosen informally, and kisses and embraces were bestowed, liberally, upon strangers, in the joyous celebration of the news of victory," reported the *News Herald*. About ninety minutes later, the band played "America" as most of the hotel's guests had crawled out of bed to join the celebration.

Mayor Osborne ordered the saloons closed at 8:00 a.m., as the revelers and those joining them from neighboring towns were whooping it up too much. The noise level reached a fever pitch as thousands of people poured into downtown Joplin to celebrate. "The forenoon and early afternoon brought forth new and fresh ideas for noise making," the *Globe* reported. "Old buckets, cans, bells, huge pieces of tin and sheet iron were attached to automobiles and dragged through the streets; pans and big strips of sheet iron were pounded and base [*sic*] drums were beaten; tin horns, paper horns and brass horns intermingled with motor horns to make up the bedlam."

The afternoon was capped by a huge parade consisting of a long line of motor cars, hundreds of people carrying banners and flags, bands, home guards, floats and a huge bell from Picher, Oklahoma, that rang continuously. Baxter Springs, Kansas, sixteen miles west, sent its entire automobile parade of three hundred motor cars to Joplin, leaving the town virtually deserted.

The Connor towers over downtown Joplin in this May 1919 photo, which shows a steady stream of trolleys rolling down Main Street. *Joplin Historical & Mineral Museum.*

The merrymaking continued far into the night, although some of it was a bit more refined. The community chorus, 150 voices strong, sang several songs from the stairs leading from the Connor lobby to the second floor.

To end the year, the Connor hosted another of its famous watch parties in the Winter Garden. For three dollars, the extravaganza included dinner at 9:30 p.m., music, noise and fun. Just minutes before the clock struck the midnight hour, "Father Time"—someone feeble and gray and carrying a long scythe—passed among the diners and climbed the stage. The lights flashed "1918," and then the Winter Garden plunged into darkness for a moment. As the lights changed to "1919," a small child—dressed in pink and carrying a bow and arrow—walked down the stage. From a distance, a chorus of horns, whistles, bells and buzzers could be heard for a solid fifteen minutes.

BARNEY ALLIS

Although it was considered a promotion, John W. Howell wasn't very happy when T.B. Baker informed him in March 1921 that he would be leaving Joplin to become Baker's traveling auditor and field representative at his hotels in Texas. Baker had persuaded Howell to move to Texas once before, in August 1918, but that had lasted only a few weeks. Howell's wife and two young daughters quickly became homesick, and Baker allowed him to return to the Connor as its manager.

Howell pitched an interesting idea to Baker: sell him the Connor instead. This would allow Howell to return to Joplin, which he now considered his permanent home. Baker initially was reluctant, as the hotel was dear to his heart. He had operated it for eleven years, and it had been his first big venture.

After a month of negotiations, Howell convinced Baker to sell him and his two partners the lease on the Connor for $200,000. Baker had recently sold his other hotel in Missouri—the Planter's House Hotel in St. Louis—and decided to concentrate on the St. Anthony and Menger in San Antonio and The Texas of Fort Worth, a fifteen-story, six-hundred-room hotel due to open in October. "I want to have my interests all close, where I can look after them without so much travel," Baker told the *Globe*.

Howell's partners were two Kansas Citians: Frank J. Dean, whose father and uncle opened the Connor in 1908, and Barney Allis, part owner of hotels in Columbia, Missouri, and Kansas City, Kansas. When his father, Delevan

James Dean, died at the age of fifty-one in 1911, Frank—then only twenty-four years old—became president of the Dean Hotel Company and took charge of running the Hotel Baltimore in Kansas City. He found the pressure too much and, suffering from a nervous disorder, took his doctor's suggestion and sold all of his stock in the hotel in 1916. The partnership with Howell and Allis five years later was Dean's first foray back into the hotel business.

The son of a Russian-born father and a Polish-born mother, Barney L. Alisky was born in Poland in 1886. His father moved the family to Kansas City when Barney was

Barney Allis. *Find a Grave.*

two, and Barney found himself hawking newspapers on a street corner four years later to help support his six brothers and sisters. He attended school through only the fourth grade and became a messenger in a downtown print shop at the age of twelve. His work ethic brought about a promotion to apprentice printer and then journeyman printer within four or five years.

When Barney was seventeen, he answered an ad in the *Kansas City Star* for "[a] young man familiar with the printing business." The job was manager of the Kansas City Bill of Fare Press, which printed daily menus for hotels and cafés. It paid less than what he was currently earning, but he accepted as he preferred the title to the money. The owner returned to Chicago, where he ran a similar business, and left Barney completely in charge. He soon became a partner and eventually bought the other man out.

As editor of *Tavern Talk*, which published every Saturday, Barney learned the hotel business by visiting hoteliers and selling them advertising. Eager to begin practicing what he had learned, Barney and a partner named Frank W. Leonard, manager of the Sexton Hotel in Kansas City, leased the newly constructed Daniel Boone Tavern in Columbia, Missouri, in 1917.

Barney made another change in his life the next year. Together with his parents, they went to court to drop the "ky" from the end of Alisky and add another "l" to become Allis. Barney never cared for the Russian-Polish suffix, figuring that it sounded un-American and hampered his business opportunities. He was also self-conscious about his height; he stood only five feet, three inches tall. The *Daily National Hotel Reporter* once referred to him as being "built close to the ground."

In 1921, Barney changed the name of his Kansas City Bill of Fare Press to the Allis Press, as "it was not properly descriptive of our business." He and Leonard purchased the Grund Hotel of Kansas City, Kansas, and formed the City Hotel Company of Kansas City with Allis as president and Leonard as vice-president. They also owned the Columbia Hotel Company, which operated the Daniel Boone Tavern, with Leonard as president and Allis as vice-president.

The most important development of 1921, however, was the Dean-Allis-Howell purchase of the Connor lease for $200,000. Dean would serve as president of the new company, Allis vice-president and Howell secretary and general manager.

Allis's influence as a promoter was immediately felt, as the Connor owners put up one hundred billboards in a fifty-mile radius of Joplin. Each sign featured a picture of the hotel and the number of miles to Joplin. The hotel also erected a large electric sign that reached from the third story to the eighth story on the southeast corner of the building. When illuminated at night, the sign could be seen from both directions on Main Street and Fourth Street.

After owning two-thirds of the Connor lease for only eighteen months, Allis and Dean surprised everyone by selling their capital stock to Howell and James M. Leonard in November 1922. For the first time in its fourteen-year history, the hotel would be owned, operated and managed by Joplin businessmen. Leonard had always been interested in the property; he had pledged $2,500 to Tom Connor in 1906 to help with the construction. One of Joplin's wealthiest citizens, he had made his fortune by buying and developing mining lands and acquiring other real estate. Leonard had also owned a banana plantation in Nicaragua, gold mines in New Mexico and oil reserves in Oklahoma.

The new owners assumed the thirty-year lease of the Dean-Allis-Howell Company and changed the name to the Leonard-Howell Company, with Howell president and general manager and Leonard vice-president. The hotel building was still owned by the Connor Investment Company, made up of the five surviving heirs of Tom Connor. Tom's nephew, Thomas Connor Nolan, had died at the age of thirty-nine of an intestinal disorder on a business trip to Kansas City in 1919.

Leonard apparently had no stomach for the hotel business, as he sold his shares back to Allis in November 1923. The corporation's name was changed to the Allis-Howell Company, with Allis president and Howell vice-president and general manager.

Howell sold his shares to Allis in April 1924, the fourth time in three years that the hotel had changed hands. Allis tried to reassure everyone that this would be the last time. "There will be no more changes in ownership," he told the *News Herald*. "I am going to live and die with this business."

To replace Howell as resident manager of the Connor, Allis hired Otto Bismarck Yetchkee (who wisely went by the initials O.B.), who had twenty-five years of experience in the hotel and catering business. He did a first-rate job in Joplin and even drew the praise of former Michigan governor Chase Osborn in May 1925 when he came to town to speak to the Pathfinder Club. "The Connor is the best managed hotel in the world," Osborn wrote to Yetchkee after his visit. "You are the manager."

When Allis took over the Connor for the second time in 1923, he commissioned a study that showed that the fifteen-year-old hotel was only 55 percent "modern." He spent more than $50,000 to completely modernize the hotel, which included rebuilding walls and bathrooms, installing new carpeting, purchasing new linens and even re-stuffing mattresses and pillows. The four-year project resulted in the Connor becoming 100 percent modernized in every respect by 1927.

"Our dream is to keep the Connor the mecca for the hotel business of this part of the southwest," Allis explained. "After all, we have nothing but service to sell, and like any manufacturing or industrial institution, we strive to turn out a finished product. Every employee in our organization constantly is being instructed in the fine parts of service. Our effort is to speed the departing guest with a pleasant memory of his stay. We intend to always keep the Connor the monument its builder intended it to be."

Although he admitted that the hotel had had fewer than ten full-capacity nights since he had owned it, Allis announced in 1927 that he would build a 152-room annex to the west of the Connor. He anticipated that the additional rooms would be needed as Joplin cemented its reputation as a convention city. It would mean that Joplin would be the only city in the country with a population of thirty-five thousand that had a four-hundred-bed hotel.

Talk of an annex to the Connor was nothing new. The idea first surfaced a dozen years before, when miners pouring into Joplin looking for work were often forced to sit up all night in chairs in the Connor lobby due to a shortage of hotel rooms. The Baker brothers aggressively pursued an eight-story, 160-room annex in 1916, but a feud between the Connor heirs eventually derailed the $500,000 project.

The Allis Hotel Company began buying up various properties around Fourth and Joplin in 1927 to make room for the annex. When Allis purchased a lot from the Connor Investment Company, it meant that his company rather than the Connor heirs would pay for and own the annex. To help raise the anticipated $600,000 cost, he sold $200,000 worth of preferred stock, paying 7 percent dividends. The stock sold for $100 per share.

"We feel that construction of this addition to the hotel marks a new era in Joplin's development and prosperity, just as erection of the original hotel celebrated the opening of a new era in the city's growth," Allis announced on January 20, 1928. "Once more the city is 20 years ahead in hotel facilities and this is our testimonial of our faith in the future of the city. Joplin and the district are steadily building up, and a population of 50,000 is no longer a remote possibility."

To design the annex, Allis hired Kansas City architect Alonzo Gentry. His fame would come later, as his projects included Municipal Auditorium (1934–35) and the Harry S. Truman Presidential Library and Museum (1955–57). Gentry's chief designer and project supervisor was Edward Voskamp, a 1916 graduate of Joplin High School who had studied in the office of architect Alfred Michaelis while in high school. Michaelis, who designed Memorial Hall in Joplin with his brother, August, died in a fifty-foot fall at Memorial Hall in 1925 while doing a final inspection of the building.

The Connor annex would have nine floors but would not be taller than the existing eight-story hotel. The extra floor would be built between the first and second floors of the current hotel, with all the hallways joining together seamlessly. Allis emphasized the fact that the entire structure would have the appearance of one huge hotel rather than a hotel and an annex. The new hotel would have 400 rooms, with the annex adding 154 of them. Each room would have a private lavatory and toilet, and most would have a private bath.

Buoyed by the success he was having in Joplin, Allis bought the lease on the Hotel Baltimore in Kansas City eleven days later. Between the Connor annex and the Baltimore purchase, he was on the hook for $1 million. He sold the Allis Press and *Tavern Talk* to reduce his outlay, but more importantly, he was now exclusively in the hotel business. For the next thirty-four years, he would be regarded as the top hotelier in the Midwest.

"Our purchase of the Baltimore Hotel makes Joplin headquarters for one of the largest hotel companies in the middle west, and gives it a new distinction as a business and commercial center," Allis told the *News Herald* in announcing the deal. "Not only that, but it will give Joplinites a home in Kansas City, a place where they will receive special courtesies and special service."

With five hundred rooms, the Baltimore was the largest hotel in Kansas City. Allis promoted the fact that Joplinites could make reservations for the Baltimore at the Connor front desk or directly with manager Herbert Simon. For guests traveling by automobile, the Baltimore's doorman would assist them with nearby garage connections. They could also take in a performance at the Shubert Theatre, two blocks from the Baltimore, and Simon could even arrange for their tickets.

Allis created a sales division within the Allis Hotel Company in March 1928 to take advantage of the fact that the two hotels would have a combined nine hundred rooms when the annex was completed. He believed that they would make ideal convention sites and that Joplin alone could attract up to one hundred large state conventions every year if the city marketed itself properly. Allis began advocating for the Joplin Chamber of Commerce to establish a convention bureau and pledged that his company would support it financially.

The hotelier was as much a publicity hound as an entrepreneur. He hit on the idea of flying 150 live rainbow trout from the Ozark Trout Farm north of Neosho to Kansas City for the formal opening of the Pompeian Room café at the Baltimore. The fish were to be placed in a fountain, where guests could select their favorite for lunch or dinner.

The event turned out to be quite a spectacle, as Paramount News sent a cameraman to the trout farm of Webster and Alice Carney the day before to show the thousands of fish. The cameraman took footage of the plane's arrival at the Joplin Municipal Airport the next morning, the loading of the fish in four ten-gallon milk cans filled with ice water and the plane's departure. Another cameraman met the plane in Kansas City and filmed the unloading and the placement of the fish in the fountain. Paramount produced a newsreel that was shown in theaters around the country.

Captain C.A. Dieter, now sixty-eight years old and regarded as the dean of Joplin builders, was awarded the annex construction contract with a bid of $400,000. Since building the original Connor Hotel twenty years earlier, he had served as general contractor for the new Joplin High School at Eighth and Wall, the Joplin National Bank Building across the street from the Connor, an addition to St. John's Hospital at Twenty-Second and Connor and numerous federal buildings.

Nearly all of the subcontractors were also Joplin firms. The H.B. Schulte Plumbing & Heating Company, with a bid of $86,321.22, received the plumbing, heating and ventilation contract. One of Schulte's challenges was installing an ice water circulating system so that every guest room could have running ice water.

The biggest hurdle remaining was linking the original hotel to the annex, making sure that all of the passageways lined up seamlessly. This required opening up the west wall of the 1908 Connor at each floor level. The original lobby was also remodeled, creating space for a women's restroom, a beauty parlor and another shop.

Allis himself designed a unique feature of the new hotel's coffee shop, the Kit Kat. Called "contabs," the four combination counters/tables were made of marble and seated four people on each side. An attendant would have water, glasses, silverware and napkins at her disposal to quickly serve her "contab" of eight people. Allis thought the "contabs" would replace the long café counters and result in faster service. He even patented his new invention.

Allis also spent $5,000 to install an elaborate public address system in the hotel. Controlled from a radio room on the roof, the system could pick up radio programs from across the country and reamplify them to all of the Connor's dining and banquet rooms and other public spaces. The radio set could also broadcast speeches, events such as heavyweight boxing matches and music provided by orchestras playing in the hotel. To manage the apparatus, Allis hired Jack Wilkerson away from the WMBH radio station in Joplin.

To recoup some of his expenses, Allis leased a good chunk of the annex's second floor to the University Club. Primarily for college graduates, the men's club formed about eight months before the annex opened. Membership was limited to 250, but a few associate members—those without any university experience—were allowed to join. This may have been a nod to Allis, who with his fourth-grade education became an associate member. James E. Harsh, general manager of the Empire District Electric Company, was the first president. Other prominent members included George A. Spiva, E.Z. Wallower and Cowgill Blair, general manager of the *Globe*.

The University Club's quarters and $25,000 in furnishings were opulent by anyone's standards. Access was by a private marble stairway just inside the Fourth Street entrance to the annex. Members could utilize a lounge, library, kitchen, two dining rooms, a room for playing cards, a room for playing checkers or chess and restrooms. There was even an office for the club's resident manager. The lounge, also known as the "main living room," contained leather chairs and a faux fireplace; the larger dining room boasted imported Viennese chairs. Although women were not generally allowed in, a "retiring room" for female guests had a dressing table, sofa and lounge.

To celebrate the opening, the 215 members of the University Club held a dance party on Thursday evening, January 31, 1929—two days before the formal unveiling of the annex. Some 500 people crowded into the adjoining Empire Ballroom and danced to music provided by the Walter Wellep Orchestra. It was the first time that wives, girlfriends and mothers were allowed to visit the club's suites, as the club's constitution and bylaws prohibited female visitors except on special occasions.

The gold and crystal Empire Ballroom featured an unusually high ceiling, six chandeliers imported from a small village in the Czech Republic and an orchestra pit set into a balcony. The room, which seated 250, also had a ventilation system that could supply fresh air at any desired temperature.

The remodeled and redecorated Roof Garden was renamed the Bal Moderne, with a capacity of 500 people for banquet purposes and even more for dances. With the Colonial Room (150), the Gold Room (75) and a few smaller meeting rooms, the Connor was now an ideal convention hotel.

The price tag had jumped from the estimated $600,000 all the way to $1 million—$800,000 for the annex and another $200,000 for remodeling and redecorating the older portion. Allis justified the cost to his stockholders by claiming that he had made "a 1910 hotel into a 1950 hotel." Eager to show off his creation, he invited the stockholders, city officials, the president and secretary of the chamber of commerce, the presidents of all the city's civic clubs and representatives from the *Globe* and *News Herald* to a luncheon in the Empire Ballroom a few days before the annex officially opened. He personally led a tour of the building after the meal.

The formal opening came on Saturday, February 2. Allis scheduled two six-course formal dinners to run simultaneously—a private one for one hundred distinguished hoteliers and his closest friends in the Marie Antoinette Dining Room and the other for two hundred invited guests in the Empire Ballroom. The menu included stuffed crab ravigote, turtle soup, Ozark rainbow trout, breast of chicken, Virginia Parisian potatoes, petit pois à la Français, Marie Antoinette salad, Swedish wafers, ice cream and petit fours. The Walter Wellep and Wayne Cox orchestras provided the music for the dinners and for a dance in the Bal Moderne Roof Garden that lasted past midnight.

The annex added 160 rooms to the existing 240. Allis claimed it was now the largest commercial hotel in the country in a city the size of Joplin. There might be a few larger resort hotels in cities Joplin's size or smaller, but they were few and far between. The "Greater Connor Hotel" was now worth $2.5 million, according to its owner.

The four hundred rooms were divided into various price categories. There were seventy-one of the lowest-priced rooms, at $2 per night, which had a toilet and lavatory but no bathtub. Rooms costing $2.50 and $3 had tiled bathrooms, with the latter being a little larger and more richly furnished. The still-larger corner rooms were $3.50 and $4 and had twin beds and more pieces of furniture. The hotel said it could house more than one thousand guests at any one time if all the rooms were fully utilized. The *Joplin Globe* was delivered to every room every morning.

A state suite on the west end of the annex's eighth floor contained a large living room and bedroom, two bathrooms, two "unusually large" closets, overstuffed chairs, marble-topped Italian coffee tables, a writing table finished in Chinese lacquer and numerous paintings. The national American Legion commander, from Indianapolis, was one of the first to stay in the state suite, as was the imperial potentate of the Shriners.

The Connor had five restaurants with regular service: the Kit Kat, Marie Antoinette, Union Bus Terminal lunch room (later called the Pup Lunch), a tea room and the University Club. It had six private dining rooms with catered service: the Colonial Room, Gold Room, Fraternity Room, Empire Ballroom, Bal Moderne and Parlor A. The Kit Kat had a seating capacity of three hundred, the Marie Antoinette one hundred and the tea room seventy.

Served by five bus lines, the Union Bus Terminal at the northwest corner of the annex made it easy for guests to arrive. There was also a parking lot on the north side for loading and unloading the buses. Guests were not allowed to park there, but attendants would take their cars to a nearby garage, where they would be washed, greased and refueled. A mechanic on duty would provide any minor repairs after consulting with the guest by telephone. When the guest was ready to leave, the valet service had the car waiting at the hotel.

There was also space for several businesses and shops along the grand corridor of the annex, which led to the bus station. These included the Citizens Loan and Investment Company, Domino Beauty Shoppe, a cigar store, a ticket office of the Kansas City Southern Railroad, Wise & Smoot investment bankers and the Bookseller. The Bookseller sold more than just books; it also offered such gifts as handkerchiefs, pillows, playing cards and costume jewelry. It even sold one-dollar memberships to its circulating library, where patrons could pay three cents per day for the latest novel.

Allis said the Greater Connor's payroll would number nearly three hundred when it was fully operational. The hierarchy included Herbert Simon, the manager; Grover C. James, secretary and attorney for the Allis

"SUNSHINE" CUTHER, HEADWAITER

For fifty years, Charles William Cuther flashed a ready smile at Connor Hotel diners, earning him the nickname of "Sunshine."

Hired by T.B. Baker in 1910, Cuther served as headwaiter until his death on Thanksgiving Day 1960. "I heard Joplin was a going concern with lots of money and a fine new hotel second to none in the country," he said in a 1956 interview of his decision to leave Dallas.

"Sunshine" worked the main dining rooms, private parties for the "rich people" and countless civic club luncheons. Although he wasn't a member, the Rotary Club recognized him in 1937 for serving 711 consecutive meetings. He also brought meals to the celebrities who stayed at the Connor—most of them preferred to dine in the privacy of their suites—and even came back in the evenings to serve them.

When black entertainers such as Duke Ellington or Marian Anderson came to Joplin, they stayed in Cuther's home, as all the city hotels were still segregated.

In 1916, "Sunshine" married Melissa Fuell, one of the most remarkable women in the city's history. A graduate of the Lincoln Institute (now Lincoln University) in Jefferson City, she taught first grade for seven years at the black Lincoln School in Joplin. She left to join the Blind Boone Concert Company as a singer and a secretary and even wrote a biography of the popular Missouri pianist and composer the year before she married.

When Paul Ewert, a former Joplin attorney and mine operator, bought the land for a park for Joplin's black population in 1924, Melissa became Ewert Park's first manager and concessionaire. She established a nursery school and kindergarten in Ewert Park and the first Girl Scout troop for black girls, was chair of the Missouri Association of Colored Women and helped create the George Washington Carver National Monument in 1953.

"Sunshine" was no slouch to public service himself, organizing Emancipation Day celebrations in Joplin for several years. More than one thousand district residents—sometimes as many as two thousand—would come to Joplin every August for parades, concerts, picnics, barbecues, swimming meets, baseball games, tennis tournaments, boxing matches, speechmaking, all-night dances and praise services.

Hotel Company; and George Wadleigh, assistant secretary, who was in charge of renting the shop space in the annex and older section. The Connor also employed an auditor, assistant auditor, stenographer, senior desk clerk, two other desk men, two cashiers, maître d'hôtel, headwaiter, chef, baker and pastry cook, chief engineer, head housekeeper, resident manager of the University Club, laundry manager, public address system operator, head bellman and barbershop manager.

Two weeks after the annex opened, the Joplin Chamber of Commerce provided Allis with one of the best evenings of his life in a banquet at his own hotel. The more than two hundred businessmen in attendance, realizing the magnitude of his accomplishment, gave him a lengthy standing ovation. "It took a reckless courage to risk a good part of your personal fortune in this enterprise, and you must love the city and its people and have all the confidence in the world in them to take the risk," said Philip Coldren, editorial page editor of the *Globe*, who served as spokesman for the group. "They say you are a dreamer. We thank God for that, for the world was built by dreamers. Amidst the plaster and debris you held a vision ever before you. That vision became a reality on opening night when your hotel became an Aladdin palace of roses, of music, of glittering corridors and laughing, happy people."

Although he still maintained an office in the Connor, Joplin would see much less of Allis for the next seventeen years. He immediately turned his attention 180 miles west, to Wichita. By August 1929, he had completed plans to build a seventeen-story, 350-room hotel that would be the tallest building in Kansas.

With its Art Deco design, the Allis Hotel was said to be patterned after New York's Waldorf Astoria. The inside, though, more closely resembled the Connor, with its grand ballroom, five private function rooms of various sizes, period furniture, barbershop, beauty parlor and three restaurants— one was even called the Kit Kat Coffee Shop. The hotel opened to the public on December 3, 1930, at a reported cost of $1.5 million.

His work done in Wichita, Allis then turned his attention back to Kansas City. His Hotel Baltimore was in the throes of a Depression-induced funk, and he tried reducing the prices on three hundred of its choicest rooms to stimulate business. Finally realizing that the Hotel Baltimore's days were numbered, Allis unloaded it in 1931 and never set foot inside again. (He reportedly had a phobia about not returning to a hotel he had sold, as it represented a failure on his part.) He turned out to be correct about the Baltimore: it was closed in 1938 and demolished one year later.

Allis had one more major project to complete at the Connor: the Rendezvous cocktail lounge. Although his Hotel Muehlebach in Kansas City (which he had acquired in 1932) had a similarly named lounge, Allis wanted something much grander for the nightspot at the Connor. He toured several hotels on the East Coast before settling on a bold theme for Joplin's Rendezvous and hiring the Kansas City architectural firm of Gentry, Voskamp and Neville, which had designed the Connor annex a decade earlier.

The most striking feature was an ornate entrance at Fourth and Main, south of the hotel entrance, with a revolving door. The Rendezvous also had three other entrances—off the main hotel lobby, off Fourth Street and from the Kit Kat. The barroom and lounge were stained in white pine, individual "opera" chairs were used in the booths, the semicircular bar was made of stainless steel and the walls were decorated with paintings by the Bavarian-born muralist John William Orth. The floor was covered by a new type of

President Harry S Truman walks through the doorway of the Hotel Muehlebach in Kansas City with Barney Allis (*right*) on November 1, 1948. *AP photo/William P. Straeter.*

rubber tile that helped to diminish noise, and the ceiling had an acoustical device that absorbed 85 percent of all sound and eliminated all sharp noises.

It seems pretty routine today, but Allis claimed that the Rendezvous's "food island" was the first to be installed in any cocktail lounge in the country. Guests could help themselves to hot and cold food, including pastries, or order off a menu. The Rendezvous also specialized in draught beer, using a refrigeration and forced air system in the basement directly below the bar.

Allis invested $80,000 in his newest creation. He was on hand to greet the hundreds who visited during the grand opening on December 22, 1938. Two years later, he installed a moveable hardwood dance floor similar to the ones used by several Chicago hotels and the Hotel Statler in St. Louis. Allis had one more innovation in mind: in March 1942, he had a leather door installed between the Rendezvous and the Kit Kat. When there was an overflow crowd in the former, the accordion-style door could be opened so the latter could be used as additional space. The door was red on the Rendezvous side and a greenish cream on the Kit Kat side to match the color schemes of both spaces.

Allis spent another $15,000 to convert unoccupied space to a barroom to accommodate the hundreds of soldiers from Camp Crowder who were spending their free time in Joplin. The Hut had a South Pacific theme— bamboo huts with thatched roofs and oak benches, fishing nets, palm leaves, seashells, a canopy and "soft, moonlike lighting." A twenty-foot bar ensured that the soldiers didn't go away thirsty.

Within a few years, Allis would devote all of his time and energy into making the Muehlebach a world-class hotel. He would become a Kansas City icon and a friend of Harry Truman. The president would spend so much time in his penthouse suite at the Muehlebach that it became known as "White House West."

AT HOME AT THE CONNOR

The Connor became an apartment hotel after the annex opened in 1929. Barney Allis initially set aside fifty rooms, including eighteen two- and three-room suites, for permanent residents. As many as one hundred people lived there at any one time, including some of Joplin's most famous citizens.

Through its advertisements, the Connor listed these practical advantages to residential hotel life:

- *Elegantly furnished rooms and suites*
- *Availability of the Marie Antoinette Dining Room and Kit Kat Café*
- *No water, light, or heat bills*
- *Four high-speed elevators to all floors*
- *Daily maid and bellboy service*
- *Numerous specialty shops located within the building, including a barbershop and a beauty salon*
- *Rates as low as $30 per month*

If those reasons couldn't convince someone to move there, then the Connor could appeal to emotion:

- *No more worrying about heat, housekeeping or transportation.*
- *Always a cool breeze in the upper floor rooms.*
- *An address of prestige.*

Herbert Simon, the manager, wrote the copy for two convincing *Joplin Globe* ads in November 1931:

> *You DO Want Your Wife to Enjoy Life. A home, in winter, is a trial and a tribulation to many women. There's the leaky faucet and the leaky gas connection; the bedroom that's always too cold and the living room that's overheated; the eternal drudgery of preparing meals; the furnace stoking; the mud that's tramped in! All these discomforts and more are banished by a residence at Hotel Connor. Give her the luxury, ease and comfort of such a residence. The new winter rates make it inexpensive.*

> *I've Arranged for My Family's Comfort. The wife, daughter and I have decided on a little real comfort this winter. There'll be none of the inconveniences of housekeeping. The new winter rates, the elegantly appointed suites, the extra comforts of a residence at Hotel Connor have won us to the decision to live this season at "Joplin's Friendly Hotel."*

One of the wealthiest individuals to live at the Connor, even before the completion of the annex, was a pioneer mining operator named G.E. Geissinger. He had resided at the Connor four or five years before his death at the hotel at the age of eighty-five. Anna Cockrum, a cigar clerk at the hotel, had befriended Geissinger and had even saved his life during one of his heart attacks. She expected to receive a substantial portion of his estate, valued at $100,000, as did another friend—the night manager of the Yellow Cab Company, which had an office at the Connor.

Geissinger's will, drawn up nearly two years before his death on November 26, 1928, did not leave anything for Cockrum or the night manager. He had indicated his desire to include the two in a conversation with an old friend who was also an attorney shortly before his death. Cockrum ended up getting only $200, while the night manager received a leather trunk. Geissinger's nieces and nephew, all of whom lived in Pennsylvania, inherited the bulk of his estate.

Congressman Joe Manlove and his wife, Alma, lived in a bridal suite at the Connor for six years when they weren't in Washington, D.C. Manlove was elected in 1922 from the Fifteenth Congressional District, which consisted of Jasper, Newton, McDonald, Lawrence, Barton, Barry and Vernon Counties. He had been a farmer, a fruit grower and a lawyer in southwest Missouri before being appointed secretary (equivalent to executive director today) of the Ozark Playgrounds Association in 1920.

Congressman Joe Manlove. *Library of Congress.*

Manlove was a five-term Republican congressman, serving from 1923 to 1933. The Manloves' son, Almon White, a 1928 graduate of Joplin High School, where he had been a football star for the Red and Green, visited his parents at the Connor while he was on holiday breaks from the University of Missouri. White Manlove played in every game for the Missouri freshman team in 1928 and was expected to make the varsity squad the following year, but a knee injury in practice ended his football career. Whitey became close friends with a former Tigers player named Paul "Dutch" Maschoff, who had become a folk hero in Columbia when he kicked the extra point in Missouri's 7–6 win over Nebraska in 1927. Maschoff spent the 1929 Thanksgiving holiday with the Manloves at the Connor.

Nira Wright held the record for living the longest time at the Connor: thirty-eight years. She moved into a second-floor apartment in November 1928 and opened a School of Singing. For the next twenty-three years, she taught hundreds of students the finer points of vocal culture based on the methods she had learned at the Lamperti-Valda School of Singing in Paris in 1909–10. Wright moved to a nursing home in Carthage for the last four years of her life, passing away there at the age of ninety-eight in 1970.

George N. Spiva, who would make any list of Joplin's most influential and wealthiest citizens, moved to the Connor from his Colonial Revival home at 611 South Sergeant a few days before he married his secretary, Zella, in February 1931. Spiva's first wife, Bessie, had died at the home in 1926, and the new Mrs. Spiva undoubtedly didn't want to live there.

George and Zella spent nineteen years living at the Connor, mostly in room 619, but the new Mrs. Spiva longed for a home of her own. She and the Spiva Investment Company developed an exclusive subdivision called Crestwood in the northwest corner of Joplin in the late 1940s. George and Zella were supposed to live in one of the houses, at 1421 Crestwood, but his death on December 2, 1950, dashed those plans. Spiva's son, George A., purchased the $80,000 home from his father's estate in 1952.

The Connor continued to convert hotel rooms into apartments as Allis realized the benefits of higher occupancy rates even at reduced prices. He ordered fifty more suites of rooms to be rebuilt and redecorated in 1938. Permanent guests could choose from studio, "bachelor" and two-, three-, four- and five-room units. The larger apartments featured kitchenettes with four-burner stoves and an oven, breakfast bars, refrigerators, "high-pile" carpeting, Venetian blinds, dinettes and bathrooms with Azrock tile floors, built-in tubs and showers, "extraordinarily large" closets and divans that could be easily converted to a sleeping unit.

The hotel's accommodations were nice enough that even a general lived there: Walter E. Prosser, the commander of Camp Crowder, a new army post southeast of Neosho. Prosser, a West Point graduate who had served in World War I, arrived at Camp Crowder from the Panama Canal Zone in March 1942. The major general and his wife, Maude, first lived at the Big Spring Inn in Neosho and then moved to the Connor later that year.

Another Camp Crowder soldier who lived at the hotel was Tommy Bridges, a thirty-seven-year-old pitcher for the Detroit Tigers who was drafted in November 1943 and reported to the post two months later. He

General Walter E. Prosser. *Camp Crowder Collection, Missouri State Archives.*

was assigned to the signal corps replacement training center as a private, but he also coached and pitched for the Crowder baseball team. He left as a sergeant in June 1945 and rejoined the Tigers in August, needing only eight victories to reach the career milestone of two hundred. He picked up only two more but still ranks no. 46 on the list of Best Detroit Tigers of All Time as of 2020.

Josephine Rosenberg, whose father, Nathan, established a shoe store in Joplin in 1897, lived at the Connor for nearly twenty-five years. Her mother, Rose, lived there too until her death in 1953. Jo was able to walk to work at Rosenberg's Shoe Store—one of the first in the country to carry the Florsheim brand. She closed the shop at 523 Main in 1969, the same year that she was forced to leave the hotel.

Blanche Freeman was another local businesswoman who lived at the Connor. When her husband, Charles, died suddenly of a brain tumor in 1936, she took over the management of the Joplin Hardware Store at 628 Main and ran it for nineteen years. She lived at the hotel from 1943 until her death in 1960. Her older sister, Minnie Hendrickson, also lived there for four years.

Mine operator George Potter and his wife, Fay, spent the last decade of their lives in the comfort of the Connor. The Potters could have lived at their "fashionable" country home at Wildwood Ranch but preferred the conveniences of downtown Joplin. George had been vice-president of the Eagle-Picher Company's mining division, where he developed "a nose for unearthing ore."

Residential hotel life wasn't just for the elderly. A few families lived at the Connor, too, including Major Elmer Block; his wife, Mary; their two-year-old son, Edwin; and a Boston terrier named Shrapnel in 1940. Block was commandant of the Joplin and Carthage high school ROTC units.

Eventually, though, all of the permanent residents of the Connor would be abruptly forced to leave the hotel for good one summer day.

ALL ROADS LEAD TO JOPLIN

With its central location, expansive network of railroads and bus lines and the reputation of being the lead and zinc capital of the world, Joplin was ideally suited to be a convention city. Having a four-hundred-room hotel with meeting, banquet and entertainment facilities brought in hundreds of conventions and thousands of dollars to the city. Joplin marketed itself as the "Convention City of the Southwest," although such cities as Tulsa, Oklahoma City, Wichita, Little Rock, Dallas, Austin, San Antonio, Albuquerque, Santa Fe and Phoenix also laid claim to that title at various times.

But even before the addition of the annex in 1929, the Connor was a big convention draw. The hotel hosted the Democratic State Convention in February 1912, thanks to Colonel William H. Phelps of Carthage. Phelps went to the Democratic State Executive Committee meeting in St. Louis and promised committee members free lodging and meals at the new million-dollar hotel if they would agree to have the convention in Joplin. In a seventeen-to-fifteen vote by secret ballot, Joplin took the event away from St. Louis.

Rooms all over town were at a premium. The secretary of the Joplin Commercial Club—the precursor to the chamber of commerce—requested that every boardinghouse and resident in the city notify him of all available beds. "It is his intention to place the Democrats in the best rooms possible if they fail to get accommodations at the hotels," the *Joplin Morning Tribune* reported.

The 1,200 delegates who attended received "extremely attractive" badges featuring a round piece of zinc the size of a silver dollar. One side was stamped "Democratic State Convention, Joplin, Mo., February 20, 1912," with a mining operation pictured in the center. The other side featured a drawing of the Connor Hotel. The convention was held in the Auditorium on Joplin Avenue, with the floor configured in the shape of the state of Missouri. The hub of activity, though, was in the Connor lobby, where it was difficult for anyone to squeeze through the crowd.

While the highlight of the convention was the endorsement of Missouri's favorite son, Congressman Champ Clark, as the 1912 Democratic presidential nominee, it was best remembered for one of the worst blizzards in Joplin's history. A "blinding" snowstorm accompanied by a "spectacular electrical storm" began at six o'clock the morning of the convention and dumped fourteen inches of snow on the city by 1:00 p.m. The *Joplin Morning Tribune*, trying to put it into perspective, perhaps overstated, "Never before in the memory of any generation of mankind alive today has such an unusual storm visited this community, and such a strange conglomeration of elemental upheavals will probably never obtain again."

Although the storm halted streetcar and automobile traffic, it did not disrupt the convention nor the enthusiasm of the 1,200 delegates who managed to make their way to the Auditorium for the 11:30 a.m. start. The only disappointment was that many had planned to see the sights of the mining district the next day. Instead, hundreds flocked to the train depots that evening, hoping to get home ahead of schedule.

Two Frisco trains carrying one hundred St. Louis delegates departed at 8:10 p.m., making it only eighteen miles before getting stuck in a snowbank just east of Carthage. Many of the passengers had retired to their sleeping berths, expecting to wake up in St. Louis, but it took snowplows twelve hours to clear the way. No food or coffee could be found in Monett, still just forty miles from Joplin, as other stranded travelers had consumed everything. The Pullmans stalled again thirty miles east, near Republic, and had to wait four hours until neighboring farmers could shovel them out. The St. Louis Democrats finally were able to get something to eat in Springfield—a full twenty-four hours after leaving Joplin—and arrived at Union Station the following morning.

Despite the uncooperative weather, the Joplin Commercial Club was buoyed by the convention's success. The city had proven that it could handle a big crowd and find rooms for all 1,200 delegates. "It proves conclusively, Joplin men feel, that Joplin is a convention city," the *Globe* editorialized. "They feel, also, that Joplin should seek more conventions as a means of advertising this section of Missouri. Through the democratic station convention, Joplin gained advertising that was worth many thousands of dollars through the daily press of the country."

Indeed, news from the Joplin convention was carried coast to coast by such newspapers as the *Atlanta Constitution, Chicago Tribune, Los Angeles Times, New York Tribune, Philadelphia Inquirer, San Francisco Examiner* and *Washington Post*. The *Indianapolis News* even declared "All Roads Lead to Joplin" as the headline in its Missouri convention preview.

Joplin waged a ferocious fight eight years later to secure the Democratic State Convention again. Jefferson City appeared to be the frontrunner over Kansas City, Sedalia and Joplin, with the *Daily Capital News* even predicting that Joplin was "too far from the state's center" to be chosen. Kansas City also wouldn't be selected because it was the home of U.S. Senator James A. Reed, who had fallen out of favor with the party.

But by offering "every possible inducement," Joplin's chamber of commerce landed the state convention. City officials presented a $1,000 certified check for expenses to the state committee and promised that they had meeting space to accommodate such a large delegation. That almost turned out to be a promise the chamber couldn't keep.

The Connor hosted both the Democratic State Convention and the Rotary conference during the same week in April 1920. First up was the two-day Rotary conference, which brought two thousand delegates and wives from fifty-seven clubs in the Seventeenth District (Missouri, Kansas and Oklahoma).

The Connor squeezed in 150 army cots and secured additional blankets and pillows, but that made only a dent in the number who needed accommodations. The Keystone had 150 rooms, and there were thirty other hotels and boardinghouses that had anywhere from 50 rooms to 2 or 3. At least seven hundred Rotarians slept in the Pullman cars that brought them to Joplin. High-powered lights were installed in all the railroad yards so that no one would trip and fall in the darkness. Each car was labeled with the name of the city from where it came, again to avoid confusion.

Even though most of the events were held at the New Joplin Theater and the Big Horn Hall of the Inter-State Grocer Company, the Connor served as the convention headquarters. The hotel bar, which had been closed due to Prohibition, was even reopened as the Rotary Cellar with "near beer" served. "The Connor hotel is about to be the busiest place in this old world during the convention," the *Joplin Globe* speculated the day before the delegates arrived. "Virtually every club in the district will have headquarters rooms for the comfort of Rotarians and ladies and it will be the 'center of the jubilee.' Bands and jazz orchestras will be as plentiful as Bolshevists in Russia."

The Connor and the other hotels had only a day to recover before nearly 1,600 delegates from the Democratic State Convention converged on the city. The Joplin Chamber of Commerce preferred the three-year-old Joplin High School auditorium, which would seat 1,392, but the school board voted unanimously to deny the request, as it didn't want to set a precedent that "secret societies, political or religious organizations" could use the facility. Norton's Garage, at Sixth and Wall, could seat 2,500, but organizers were turned off by the grease on the floor. After deeming the New Joplin Theater too small, the chamber considered erecting a huge tent in Schifferdecker Park, but transportation issues and weather concerns ruled that out.

Desperate to find suitable space just two weeks before the delegates arrived, the chamber turned to Bernard Levy, manager of the Hippodrome theater at 517 Main. Levy reluctantly agreed to allow the Democratic State Convention to use his 1,600-seat facility for the one-day meeting on April 22. It meant a loss of revenue for Levy, who still had to pay his vaudeville performers and motion picture rental fees. The tight-fisted manager made the chamber promise that he never again would be asked to make "such a sacrifice."

The room shortage also had to be dealt with again. The chamber formed a volunteer committee of women to call those who had housed Rotary delegates and make a list of private homes willing to host the Democrats. Compounding the problem, some of the Rotarians in town for their convention stayed on and kept their rooms in order to watch the Democratic "scrap." The state committee had thirty-two rooms at the Connor, including a suite for Governor Frederick Gardner in room 509.

The hotel lobby was a "seething maelstrom" until Gardner delivered the keynote address at the Hippodrome. It was impossible to walk more than a few feet, with the crowd also filling the second-floor mezzanine and spilling out onto the sidewalk. A gubernatorial candidate named Frank Farris from Rolla, Missouri, had his khaki-clad band squeeze into the lobby and play "Dixie" and other old favorites.

Women participated for the first time as delegates at the Joplin convention, but they did not have the desired "chastening effect" on the men that many had predicted. Marguerite Martyn, who covered the event for the *Post-Dispatch*, noted that "the women, instead of injecting order, decorum, politeness, upset all these anticipations" and "were capable of hooting and howling with the best or the worst" of the men. Her other takeaway was that the female delegates held up well during the all-night session and had "all the staying power, all the patience, even greater endurance of fatigue." Martyn was surprised that on the return train ride to St. Louis, the women preferred to sit up all day and discuss the events of the night before rather than take a nap.

The Democrats did not rate the city of Joplin nearly as highly as they had eight years earlier. Delegates from northeast Missouri complained to their local newspaper that the Hippodrome was a "dimly lighted moving picture house" and that many spectators who had traveled great distances were unable to enter due to the size of the crowd. "The hotel accommodations were inadequate and the crowds suffered many inconveniences," the *Palmyra Spectator* added. The paper concluded that only two cities in the state—St. Louis and Kansas City—were properly equipped to handle such large conventions.

The *Joplin Globe* used the opportunity to editorialize for building a "real convention hall" in the city. The idea quickly gained momentum, and three years later, voters approved a $250,000 bond issue to construct a convention

After the conclusion of World War I, the American Legion began a drive to build a grand opera house and convention hall as a memorial to the national defenders who served in all branches of the military. Memorial Hall opened in 1925 at a cost of $250,000. *Joplin Historical Postcards/Joplin Public Library.*

center and a monument to the city's war heroes. Memorial Hall, with a seating capacity of 3,300, opened at Eighth and Joplin in October 1925 and enabled the city to attract numerous conventions over the next forty years.

Joplin and the Connor hosted three prominent conventions in September 1931. First up was the American Legion state convention, which brought an invasion of registered delegates, visiting auxiliary members and wives. Five days before the Legionnaires arrived, the chamber announced that 1,300 hotel reservations had been made and that it expected 3,000 delegates and visitors to come to Joplin for the three-day convention. Final attendance figures were never announced, but Kansas City alone sent a delegation that numbered more than 500—including four drum and bugle corps, two women's choral clubs and one women's drill team. The Albany, Missouri American Legion chapter reported that 8,000 attended the Joplin convention, but that number cannot be verified.

The highlight of the American Legion convention was a "mammoth" Labor Day parade attended by an estimated forty thousand. The state commander and other Legion officials observed the festivities from a viewing stand in front of the Connor. The parade had a serious undertone, however. Legion officials warned Joplin residents to lock their houses, as "professional criminals seeking to take advantage of the situation" might pay a visit during their absence.

The convention did draw an unsavory element to Joplin. There were "imposters," those ages eighteen to twenty-two who posed as members of the American Legion in order to get drunk and destroy property. There were older "tough onions," who also came to get drunk and engage in various forms of debauchery. And there were professional gamblers, including two who attacked a Connor Hotel elevator operator and knocked him unconscious. Still, local officials were pleased that there was relatively little property damage, which was often associated with Legion conventions.

Following the Legionnaires, one thousand Kiwanians and their wives made their way to Joplin for the Missouri-Kansas-Arkansas district convention. Delegates had numerous meetings at the Connor, played golf at Schifferdecker and Oak Hill, attended informal theater parties, took sightseeing trips of Joplin and the vicinity and had a banquet and ball at the Scottish Rite Temple.

When the western division of the American Mining Congress and the American Institute of Mining and Metallurgical Engineers came to Joplin for their joint meeting, the Connor ran a huge ad in the *News Herald* boasting "Our Third Convention in as Many Weeks!" It was the smallest of the three, with some three hundred delegates and wives, but easily the biggest coup for the city. Joplin had landed the convention nearly a year earlier in competition with Salt Lake City and San Francisco. Although those cities offered better amenities, delegates preferred to see firsthand the famous Tri-State District, the heaviest producer of lead and zinc in the world.

The mining operators, engineers and geologists spent several hours at the Schifferdecker Lead and Zinc Museum, which had just opened a few months earlier. They also enjoyed a banquet featuring dancing and vaudeville on the Connor's Bal Moderne rooftop, but the biggest highlight was an all-day field trip to inspect mines in Kansas and Oklahoma. A caravan of fifty automobiles left the hotel at 9:00 a.m. and visited mining sites in Galena, Baxter Springs, Picher and Cardin—including the famous Blue Goose, where the cars were able to drive down into the mine. Following a barbecue and rodeo in Miami, Oklahoma, the weary visitors returned to the Connor for a good night's sleep.

The conventions continued to pour into Joplin. The chamber reported in April 1932 that the city had hosted 101 conventions or similar meetings in the past year, bringing in an estimated eighteen thousand visitors with a total expenditure of $600,000. Joplin beat out Kansas City, St. Louis, Columbia and Excelsior Springs in landing the 1932 Missouri Pharmaceutical Association convention in June. The entire mezzanine floor of the Connor was turned over into a complete display of drugstore merchandise.

Hosting the 1936 Democratic State Convention taxed the city's resources to the fullest degree. St. Louis, Cape Girardeau and Springfield also sought the convention, but the executive committee voted to accept Joplin's invitation and pledge of hospitality. The *St. Louis Post-Dispatch* had no problem with the decision, saying it was always worth coming to the "Zinc Metropolis." The newspaper explained: "Joplin always has had spiritual riches, whatever it may lack in material pomp. If there are no galleries there, with musing hosts of marble, no topless towers, no Gothic glory, the city possesses a rare and radiant genius of its own. There is the atmosphere of joie de vivre, a genuine urbanity, a sure enough savior faire, an around-the-clock hospitality."

Expecting six thousand to seven thousand to come to Joplin, the chamber's housing committee put out a call for local residents to open their homes to the delegates and visitors. Upon inspection, the majority of the homes offered up were less than satisfactory, causing the committee to issue a plea for "better class" residences. Traveling salesmen were also sent notices to stay away from Joplin during the May 4–5 convention.

Hundreds of visitors ended up being housed in boardinghouses and private residences. The housing committee set up headquarters in the Connor and used Boy Scouts to escort guests from the hotel to their accommodations. Hotels fifteen miles away in Carthage and Neosho were also used, as were tourist camps in the area.

Because Memorial Hall could seat no more than 3,500 of the 5,100 delegates, the Jasper County Democratic Committee considered moving the event to Junge Stadium. The stadium had seating for roughly the same amount, but a speakers' platform and several thousand additional seats could be placed on the football field. Local residents would be asked to provide rides to and from the stadium. The idea was later scuttled due to concerns about the weather and transportation issues.

Harry Truman, then a U.S. senator, arrived two days before the convention and stayed in a suite at the Connor. The *Joplin Globe* published a picture of Truman having a Sunday evening dinner at the hotel with three other party officials. Kansas City political boss Tom Pendergast was in Europe but sent his nephew and chief aide, James, to represent him. "Jimmy" Pendergast entertained numerous delegates in his headquarters at the Connor.

The delegates and visitors who arrived by train and automobile jammed the Connor lobby and every floor of the hotel the night before the convention. The hotel set up an emergency bar just off the lobby, using the doors procured from the old House of Lords saloon years earlier. As the crowd spilled out onto Main Street, another bar "employed a rasping loud speaker to entice the thirsty," according to the *St. Louis Post-Dispatch*.

While the majority engaged in frivolity, others attended private dinner parties, dances, movies and even wrestling matches at Memorial Hall. Josephine O'Connor, the widow of Jerry O'Connor—Tom Connor's nephew—hosted an afternoon tea at her home for Margaret Stark and other Democratic women. Margaret's husband, Lloyd, would be elected governor of Missouri in six months.

Expecting a crowd of 10,000 on the day of the convention, the chairman of the local transportation committee urged Joplin residents to leave their cars at home. Party officials still worried how they would be able to shoehorn 5,100 potential delegates and alternates into a building that could seat only 3,300 comfortably. They somehow managed to cram 900 more seats into Memorial Hall and then set up an amplifying system to broadcast the speeches onto the street in front. An estimated 1,000 listened on the loudspeakers.

Bennett Champ Clark, who had been elected to the U.S. Senate in 1932, gave the keynote address. The sound system inside Memorial Hall quickly malfunctioned, causing many of the delegates to shout at Clark to speak "louder." The senator became so frustrated at one point that he stopped abruptly and retorted, "If any of you boys want to make this speech for me, come on up and do it." The system later was fixed during a twenty-minute recess, but by that time at least a third of the crowd had slipped out.

The secretary of the Missouri State Democratic Committee called the Joplin convention the largest one she had experienced in her twenty years with the party. "For some reason, everybody wanted to come to Joplin for the convention this year," said Lula May Barry, who speculated that the improving economy played a major role.

The Lions Club of Missouri held its 1938 convention in Joplin, with some 700 members and Ladies of Lions attending. Those staying at the Connor must have thought the place was under attack when a series of aerial bomb

Bennett Champ Clark (*right*). *Library of Congress.*

blasts interrupted their sleep early in the morning on the first day. But it was merely a stunt to signify the roaring of lions. The Connor also hosted the 136th district conference of Rotary International in 1938, with 785 "Rotes" and Rotary Anns attending from the four-state district.

Joplin experienced another banner convention year in 1939, with seventeen major conventions bringing more than thirteen thousand visitors to the city. Topping the list was a return of the state American Legion in September. The city was so concerned that things might get out of hand that it called in thirty-four highway patrolmen and several police officers from Springfield, St. Louis and Cape Girardeau to help handle the four thousand war veterans.

The Forty and Eight Society—the merrymaking arm of the Legion— may have been subdued somewhat by a record-breaking temperature of 104 but still managed to engage in plenty of frivolity. Someone mounted a toy cannon to a large automobile and fired it throughout the downtown area, rattling windows. A group from Springfield attached a machine gun and muskets from the Civil War to its car but fortunately did not set them off. The Clinton Legionnaires dressed up as Osage Indians, complete with war paint and tomahawks, while performing war dances and going on "scalping expeditions."

To combat the anticipated room shortage, the American Legion Housing Committee had placed ads in the *Globe* and *News Herald*: "Attention, Mrs. Joplin! Have You a Spare Room? We must have 500 clean sleeping rooms to house Mr. and Mrs. Legionnaire and their children." The committee suggested a price of one dollar per person per night. Cots were also set up in various locations around town.

Governor Lloyd Stark, Truman and Bennett Champ Clark participated in the Legion's big Labor Day parade and spoke at Memorial Hall. The event that drew the most attention, however, was when several Legionnaires hanged two Adolph Hitler effigies—one on a stoplight at Fourth and Main and the other from a balcony at the Connor. The first dummy wore a sign: "Hitler: the world's biggest ass." *LIFE* magazine reprinted the *News Herald* photo two weeks later.

The Young Democratic Clubs of Missouri brought 750 to Joplin for its February 24–25 convention. Landing this group was a real coup for Joplin, as the Young Democrats had met only in Kansas City, St. Louis and Jefferson City before 1939. The convention was marred by a fire that swept through the Connor at eight o'clock on Saturday evening. The fire started in rooms 408 and 409—a corner suite that had been occupied by Secretary of State

Legionnaires hang Hitler in effigy on Main Street in September 1939. *From the* Joplin News Herald.

Dwight H. Brown and two companions. The Brown party had checked out two hours earlier but apparently had left a cigar or cigarette burning.

The hotel was plunged into chaos as flames licked out the windows and dense smoke filled the upper five floors. Firefighters were quickly on the scene, using a truck with an aerial ladder to enter the building and extinguish the fire within twenty minutes. A crowd estimated at more than one thousand gathered at Fourth and Main to watch while the hundreds still inside the Connor raced down the stairs in total darkness to safety. One woman on the top floor paid a hotel employee one dollar to carry her down eight flights of stairs.

The Joplin Fire Department demonstrates how its new aerial ladder will reach the eighth floor of the Connor, with firemen at various points on the ladder, on April 15, 1939. *Joplin Historical & Mineral Museum.*

The Connor's "absolutely fireproof" construction averted a tragedy. The concrete/steel walls and floors contained the flames on the fourth floor; the primary damage was caused by the smoke and water.

In a strange twist of fate, another fire nearly five years later resulted in the death of Dwight Brown. The three-term secretary of state had just announced his candidacy for governor in December 1943 when a fire destroyed his three-story home in Jefferson City. The scantily clad Brown, who was in bed with a cold, managed to escape into the deep snow outside, but the exposure to the cold brought about a bad case of influenza.

Brown's condition worsened over the next three months, so much so that he had to drop out of the governor's race in March 1944. That opened the door for state senator Phil Donnelly, who filed for the office only a few hours after Brown's withdrawal and was elected in November. Brown died in Poplar Bluff on May 8 at the age of fifty-seven.

Conventions continued to pour into Joplin in the 1940s, although the number diminished slightly from the previous decade. The biggest one during the war years was the Southwest Missouri Teachers' Association, which brought two thousand to town in October 1943. Again the city had to deal with a housing shortage, as school administrators quickly snapped up all the hotel rooms. The convention housing committee put out a call for 1,500 rooms for teachers, suggesting a price of one dollar per night. Motion picture star Lillian Gish was the featured speaker, discussing "The Odyssey of an American Trouper" at Memorial Hall.

The number of conventions began diminishing in the 1950s. Joplin suffered a particularly bad year in 1954, hosting only nine conventions with a total attendance of 1,500. The city may not have realized it at the time, but Columbia had surpassed it as the third major convention city in the state.

Columbia hosted more than one hundred conventions and fifty thousand delegates in 1957—numbers that Joplin had never seen. Joplin's population was still slightly greater in the late 1950s, but Columbia had two distinct advantages: its location in the center of the state and the University of Missouri. The university's Division of Continuing Education, College of Agriculture, School of Journalism, athletic teams, meeting rooms and residence halls all contributed to making Columbia a more desirable location.

OH, WHAT A STRANGE MAGIC

As the heart and soul of the Joplin community for fifty years, the Connor naturally attracted more than its fair share of celebrities, daredevils, hustlers, con artists, prostitutes and other questionable characters. The hotel was also the scene of numerous stunts, demonstrations, accidents, suicides and even a bombing and a shooting.

It was an easy decision for movie stars, musicians, authors, politicians and famous athletes to stay at the Connor if they were in town for an engagement or just passing through. The hotel would provide a suite of rooms, if requested, as well as all its other amenities and its location in the heart of Joplin. Guests could also expect a certain amount of privacy.

Using the proximity to the Connor to help sell properties became standard practice soon after the hotel opened in 1908. An eleven-room residence, made of pressed brick, was five blocks west of the hotel. A modern, six-room bungalow was within a five-minute walk of the hotel. A new, well-built cottage was within thirteen blocks. An eighty-acre farm with rich soil was two and a half miles away. L.W. and Carl McDonald advertised twenty acres a mile and a half north of the Connor on North Main, the "perfect tourist cabin location."

As the tallest building in Joplin, the Connor was also the reference point for some unusual comparisons. In 1911, the Joplin Fire Department boasted that its new fire engine could shoot a stream of water sixty feet higher than the Connor. When *Globe* sports columnist Porter Wittich was trying to tell his readers in 1938 just how big the new Grand River Dam in northeast Oklahoma would be, he told them to "imagine a building three stories higher than the Connor hotel stretching from Fourth and Main to beyond Maiden Lane."

No one was more enamored of the height of the Connor than a hustler and gambler named "Titanic" Thompson. Born Alvin Clarence Thomas in Monett, Missouri, in 1892, he acquired his nickname in 1912 after running the table against Joplin pool shark Snow Clark and winning a $500 bet. As he left the Del Monte Billiard Parlor at 418 Main, Alvin noticed that Clark had posted a sign in the window: "$200 to Any Man Who Jumps over My New Pool Table." It seemed like an impossible feat, and Clark and the others laughed when Alvin swore he could do it.

Alvin returned ten minutes later, dragging an old mattress he had acquired. He placed the mattress on the other side of the pool table, took a running start and cleared the table—landing on his back on the mattress. As he counted his winnings, someone asked Clark the stranger's name. "I don't rightly know, but it ought to be Titanic," Clark said. "He sinks everybody."

Seventeen years later, when Alvin testified in a murder trial in New York, reporters mistakenly called him Thompson instead of Thomas. For the rest of his life, he was known as Titanic Thompson. Writer Damon Runyon was particularly enamored of Titanic, using him as the model for a character in his 1933 short story "The Idyll of Miss Sarah Brown." The character—gambler Sky Masterson—was one of the stars of the musical *Guys and Dolls*, based on Runyon's short story. Titanic would go on to write a lengthy account of his life in *Sports Illustrated* in 1972, and two books were published about him after his death.

But a decade or so before he sprung to national fame, Titanic spent a considerable amount of time in Joplin looking for suckers to hustle. In one instance, he purchased two dozen oranges and took them to a taxi stand near the Connor. He asked several drivers to throw one up on the hotel's roof, but no one could. The proprietor of the House of Lords pool hall, a man named "Hickory" McCullough, saw the commotion and came over. When his attempt fell far short, McCullough said no one could throw an orange that far. Titanic said he could, and McCullough accepted his offer of a $2,000 bet. McCullough, unaware that Titanic had been practicing the night before, had to pay up when the gambler's orange cleared the Connor by twenty feet.

On another occasion, Titanic bet a group of boys $500 that he could throw a pumpkin over the hotel. Much to their dismay, he produced a miniature pumpkin the size of a baseball and fired it over the roof. There was a rumor—unsubstantiated, of course—that Titanic had plugged the pumpkin with some lead.

In 1920, several Joplin promoters came up with a novel idea: hold a rock-throwing competition to determine the unofficial champion of the world. They pledged a $1,000 prize, figuring that the publicity and side bets would more than cover their investment. They selected only two contestants: Titanic and Joe Henry, a young farmer from nearby Avilla who could throw a stone across a forty-acre field on his property. Titanic, in a publicity stunt, threw a lime onto the roof of the Connor and followed it up by tossing a walnut over the top. There is no record that the contest ever took place, presumably because the prize money didn't materialize.

If people weren't trying to throw things over the Connor, then they were attempting to climb it. At least five "human flies" or "human spiders" scaled the hotel between 1915 and 1920 as this form of stunt entertainers was taking the nation by storm. As Jacob Smith explained in his *The Thrill Makers: Celebrity, Masculinity, and Stunt Performance*, "The most obvious explanation for the allure of this performance was the very real potential for the audience to witness a spectacular and horrifying death."

The first to visit Joplin was Harry Gardiner in 1915. According to several accounts, former president Grover Cleveland had proclaimed him the "Human Fly," but Gardiner also had other nicknames: the "Undertaker Dodger," the "Prince of Daredevils" and the "Grave-Digger's Friend." The coroner and an ambulance were supposedly on hand whenever he climbed a building.

Prior to coming to Joplin, Gardiner had scaled the Flatiron Building, Grant's Tomb and the Singer Tower in New York. His 1915 national tour was sponsored by the curiously named Satan-et, "the drink with a wink." The manufacturer advertised that Gardiner consumed the soft drink to steady his nerves. He had a New York–based agent and a local agent in each city to make the necessary arrangements, which often included getting permission from the municipality and the owner of the building. In Joplin, the Redell Manufacturing and Supply Company, which sold the beverage, put up a $100 bond with the city guaranteeing that the "Human Fly" would climb the Connor "or make an honest effort to do so, the weather permitting."

The *Globe* reported that nearly five thousand onlookers saw Gardiner "defy death" on May 10; many had to turn away, fearful that he would slip and fall to certain death. The consummate showman, the "Human Fly" didn't disappoint. As he reached the seventh floor and then the eighth, Gardiner clung to the window ledges by only his fingertips. Nearing the roof, he stopped and tapped on the hollow cornice, explaining to the crowd below: "The chances are 99 to one that this tin will not hold me. I am using a rope here because I am sure you would not desire to see me die." As the crowd cheered, he used a rope to pull himself up and over the roof of the hotel.

Gardiner returned to Joplin a year later for a three-day engagement at the Electric Theater, where it was billed that he would reveal how he accomplished "his marvelous feats in midair." He also climbed the Connor on Monday, the Frisco Building on Tuesday and the Jasper County Courthouse in Carthage on Wednesday—all precisely at 12:15 p.m. to attract lunchtime crowds. As he had done the year before, the "Human Fly" put on quite a show for the thousands gathered at Fourth and Main. When he reached the sixth floor, he pushed his feet away from the hotel to demonstrate that he was gripping the window ledge with only his fingertips. Upon reaching the seventh story, he let one of his hands drop free to show that he was holding on by only a few fingers. It took Gardiner thirteen minutes to climb the building and another seven to shimmy down.

Bill Strother was the most famous daredevil to climb the Connor. The actor Harold Lloyd, who dangles from the hands of a huge clock twelve stories above a busy street in the 1923 silent movie *Safety Last*, saw Strother scale a building in Los Angeles in 1922. "Well, it made such a terrific impression on me, and stirred my emotions to such a degree that I thought, 'My, if it can possibly do that to an audience—if I can capture that on the screen—I think I've got something that's never been done before,'" he said. Lloyd persuaded producer Hal Roach to sign Strother to a contract, and he appears in the movie. *Safety Last* made the American Film Institute's list of the one hundred most thrilling American films of all time.

Four years before he became an actor, Strother came to Joplin. Billed as the "Human Spider," he spoke to the large crowd at Fourth and Main before climbing the south side of the Connor. "I hold nobody responsible for my life. I may fall and break my neck, but if I do, it will be the first time." When Strother reached the sixth floor, he added a bit of theatrics, appearing to slip but grabbing the windowsill to prevent a fall. Upon reaching the top, he announced that he would climb the hotel again that evening, blindfolded, and ride a bicycle along the cornice, also blindfolded. There is no record that proves Strother accomplished this, but he had ascended the Hotel Tulsa blindfolded five days earlier.

The next "human fly" to tantalize Joplin was George Polley in May 1920. Polley's claim to fame was attempting to climb the world's tallest skyscraper, the Woolworth Building, a few months earlier. Upon reaching the thirtieth floor, with twenty-seven more to go, he had been arrested for not possessing a permit. The Hudson-Hughes Motor Company, which sponsored Polley's Joplin performances, conveniently omitted that part in a *Globe* advertisement, claiming that he "is the only man living today who has climbed the Woolworth Building, New York City—57 stories high—785 feet in the air."

Polley drove an Essex provided by Hudson-Hughes around town while he waited to climb the Connor and the Newman Building the following day. Unlike Harry Gardiner five years earlier, Polley did not use a rope to pull himself over the roof. "I am not surprised others have not tried to climb over the Connor's cornice, but it can be done," he said beforehand. "While it is a difficult job, it just takes a little nerve." Not only did he climb over the ledge sans rope, he also stood on his head atop it. And then for good measure, he shimmied up the flagpole on the roof.

Just five months later, another "human fly" brought his talents to Joplin. Weighing just slightly more than one hundred pounds, Jack Williams was known for his fingers, which were "more like steel claws than bone and flesh, as they clung and hung to the tiniest of crevices." Williams spent several days at the Connor, even placing an ad in the *News Herald* for a manager or advance agent. "A real live hustler can make three to four hundred a week or will pay the right man a reasonable salary," the ad read. "Those with publicity or newspaper experience given preference. Salesmanship counts most of all. Bums, grafters, save your time."

Williams seemed to function quite well as his own agent. He lined up four sponsors for his Joplin visit: the Hudson-Hughes Motor Company, the *News Herald*, the Joplin Tire and Rubber Company and the Lekas Confectionery and Luncheonette. Hudson-Hughes loaned him a new Essex to drive around town, providing he wear an Essex advertisement on his back during the climb. He threw copies of the *News Herald* down to the crowd; each copy was marked and redeemable for a prize at a local merchant. The tire company gave away inner tubes, and the confectionery brought Williams in immediately following to answer questions and sell candy. If that wasn't enough, the daredevil also received 70 percent of a collection taken up during his ascent. The American Legion got the rest.

It would be twenty-eight years before another "human fly" attempted to scale the Connor Hotel. At fifty-one years old, Johnnie Woods claimed to be the last one left in the business. The vegetarian had been climbing buildings for thirty-two years, his tallest being the forty-two-story Smith Tower in

Seattle. Williams climbed the Connor annex twice on Saturday, November 20, 1948, as a benefit for the Earl J. Bruton Post, Veterans of Foreign Wars. His three o'clock performance drew the largest crowd, which spread three blocks between Wall and Virginia on Fourth Street. The crowd roared as he stood on his head atop the roof. His 9:00 p.m. performance, under a spotlight in near-freezing temperatures, drew a much smaller audience.

If people weren't climbing the Connor, then they were throwing things out the windows. In 1937, a man from Long Beach, California, forced pedestrians on Fourth Street to take cover when he let loose a barrage of furniture and stone tabletops from his seventh-story window. Joplin police had to break down his door to stop the rampage and arrest him for drunkenness. A thirty-two-year-old guest from Tulsa was arrested seven years later for pitching bottles out of his seventh-floor room.

Those cases were easily solved, but others were not, such as who threw ink bottles from an upper room every so often in 1910. Or why conventioneers once tossed a live goat out of a fourth- or fifth-floor window. One of the saddest instances occurred in 1909, when a man from Oklahoma City smuggled his Boston terrier into his seventh-floor room. When the dog noticed his master on the street below, it leaped out the window to its death, causing a bystander to faint.

Unfortunately, the Connor was also the scene of several suicides. There wasn't a more tragic figure than Maggie Morgan, who jumped to her death from her eighth-story window on October 11, 1930. Maggie's life revolved around her Neosho veterinarian husband, Dr. David Benjamin Morgan. When they were married in 1914, the local newspaper declared that he was "probably known by more people than any other man in Southwest Missouri." Maggie accompanied him on many of his visits to treat sick and injured animals, including one to McDonald County on a Sunday afternoon in late September. Dr. Morgan became seriously ill on the way home and died soon after of coronary heart disease.

The grief-stricken Maggie, who had no living relatives except for her husband's, told a friend ten days after his funeral that she would be away from home for a few days, perhaps traveling to Kansas City. Instead, she checked into the Connor Hotel, where she had many happy memories from the numerous times the couple had stayed there. Maggie was a woman determined to end her own life: she brought poison to the room and slashed her throat, wrists and femoral artery before jumping. She left a brief note, indicating that she wanted her estate to go to her husband's brother and two sisters.

There was at least one other suicide from jumping off the Connor, in 1945. A thirty-eight-year-old Iowa man who had received a medical discharge from the navy only two months earlier, "though he was anything but a well man," according to his hometown newspaper, stopped at the hotel en route to visit his father in Texas. Robert Mitcham jumped from his fourth-floor room in the annex in the middle of the night and was able to tell Joplin police that he had intended to end his life before being taken to St. John's Hospital. He died the following day, with the *Chariton (IA) Herald Patriot* calling him "another of the many casualties of war."

There were numerous suicides in Joplin, to be sure, but none seem to capture the public's attention as much as those that occurred at the Connor. In 1910, a twenty-three-year-old stenographer from Altamont, Kansas, disappeared from her sister's house at Twenty-Second and Sergeant Avenue in Joplin. Mabel Harrington left her purse containing fifty dollars but did take her brother-in-law's revolver. While the family searched, even offering a twenty-five-dollar reward, Mabel had checked into an eighth-story room at the Connor. T.B. Baker, manager of the hotel, noticed her sitting at a writing desk in a second-floor parlor the following day but was unaware that she had been reported missing. Baker would have taken immediate action if he had known that Mabel was writing a suicide note to her mother.

Mabel blamed consumption (tuberculosis) and the weakened state it had left her in for her decision to end her life. She pinned the note to her clothing and then fired the revolver. If anyone in the hotel heard the shot, they must have assumed that it was a mine blast or the excavation of the Joplin Union Depot building site a few blocks away. She wasn't found for about twenty-four hours.

When he retired as bell captain in 1962 after fifty-two years of service, Ward Provance said there had been at least ten suicides at the hotel. "Never will I forget the day the nice-looking lady rented a room on the eighth floor," he said, perhaps remembering the 1930 death of Maggie Morgan. Provance was one of three Connor employees who found her body. "She ordered a chocolate malt, drank it, opened the window and jumped out. Another time I had to crawl through the transom of the locked door to see why this man had not left his room for three days. He'd taken poison."

Aside from suicides, heart attacks and drownings in bathtubs brought on by heart attacks, the most common type of death at the Connor involved elevators. At least three men died of fractured skulls from falling down elevator shafts or being struck by elevators. Clarence Arnold, a twenty-five-year-old busboy at the Pup Lunch, unlocked the door to the elevator shaft, apparently planning to walk across the elevator to a corridor leading to the kitchen. The elevator, however, was not on the first floor but in the basement.

One year later, in 1935, the delivery superintendent for Miners Ice and Fuel Company and two others were inspecting room air conditioners on the second floor of the hotel. James Spain, forty-nine, rang for the elevator; thinking it was on the first floor, he peered down into the shaft. The elevator was on the floor above, however, and struck him near the base of his skull as it descended.

A forty-seven-year-old bellman unlocked the elevator doors at 2:00 a.m. on a September Sunday in 1944, expecting the elevator to be there. Merl Ferguson stepped into the darkened shaft and fell eighteen feet from the first floor into the elevator pit. He wasn't discovered for five and a half hours, when Provance came on duty and was informed that he was missing. Remembering that Arnold's body had been discovered in the pit ten years earlier, Provance called down and heard Ferguson moaning. He died forty hours later, never regaining consciousness.

As the center of Joplin's universe, the Connor was the place where individuals or groups could go to make a political statement or get some free publicity. The most egregious example occurred in 1923, when nine robed members of the Ku Klux Klan marched into a hospital fundraising dinner in the hotel and presented sacks of coins and stacks of bills totaling $10,086. The Klansmen presented a letter of explanation along with their donation and stood silently while the letter was read aloud. They even posed for a picture along with some of the dinner attendees and three black waiters before taking the elevator to the lobby and marching single file out to two waiting cars.

The Klan's appearance at the Connor was a carefully orchestrated plan, with the nine men entering the hotel in regular clothes and finding an empty room to change into their robes. The getaway cars took them to Fairview Cemetery, where two other autos capable of high speeds were waiting to whisk them out of the city. Including the $10,000 from the KKK, Joplin-area citizens raised $125,000 toward the construction of Freeman Hospital, which opened in 1925. Ozark Klan No. 3—with members in Joplin, Webb City, Carl Junction, Oronogo, Alba, Neck City, Purcell, Waco, Asbury and some rural areas—gave the lion's share of the money, but members in Kansas and Oklahoma also chipped in.

The Connor was at the forefront of another public demonstration two decades later. A strike by milk truck drivers and other union employees against the Gateway Creamery Company in 1946 initially resulted in

Ku Klux Klan Gives $10,086 to Hospital Fund

In the midst of a dinner on the Connor hotel roof Friday night, when workers in the $125,000 campaign for Freeman Memorial hospital were meeting for reports on the progress of the drive, nine robed Klansmen appeared and deposited $10,086 in cash on the table as a donation to the fund. Ozark Klan No. 3, which includes members from Joplin, Webb City, Carl Junction, Asbury, Oronogo, Alba, Purcell, Waco, Neck City and contiguous territory, gave $9,576 of the amount; the Cardin, Okla., Klan gave $100; Galena Klan, $300; and individual Klansmen in Ottawa county, Oklahoma, gave $110. An error was made in The Globe's article yesterday morning, when it was stated the Galena, Klan's donation was $100. M. Gosting, photographer, made a flashlight picture of the scene before the Klansmen departed. Negro waiters in the room at the time remained and posed with the Klansmen and campaign workers. The Klansmen then left the hotel by way of the main elevator, walking through the lobby to two motor cars that had been parked in front of the hotel, and drove away.

Nine robed Klansmen appeared at a fundraising dinner on the Connor roof in June 1923 and deposited $10,086 in cash toward a drive for a new hospital. *From the* Joplin Globe.

picketing against businesses that purchased Gateway milk and ice cream products. It quickly turned ugly, with stink bombs tossed into three grocery stores, mustard oil poured on a horse that pulled a Gateway delivery wagon, acts of sabotage against company machinery and milk bottles being smashed upon arrival at a Kresge store.

A restraining order from a circuit court judge quelled some of the violence, but an overzealous striker named John Henry Bankhead decided to take matters into his own hands. Bankhead had shot and killed a man three years earlier while serving as police chief of nearby Galena, Kansas. The man, who had stolen a watch from a resident, fired a bullet into Bankhead's back—puncturing his lung—before the chief returned the fire. A coroner's jury found that he had acted in self-defense. Bankhead was never quite the same afterward and bounced around at various jobs before ending up at Gateway Creamery.

As the strike continued into its third month, Bankhead became incensed that local establishments were still purchasing Gateway milk and ice cream. The Connor, with its Rendezvous and Kit Kat restaurants, was among the biggest offenders. The union president even visited the hotel's manager, J.J. Dewey, and threatened to post a picket line in front of the building if the hotel persisted. Shortly before noon on Saturday, August 17, when the Connor was at its busiest, Bankhead entered the lobby and smashed four stink bombs in various places. As guests scurried outside to avoid the odor, Bankhead escaped through the Fourth Street entrance to a waiting getaway car.

Bankhead was arrested three days later, after two waitresses and another employee identified him as the culprit. One of the waitresses testified that Bankhead had almost collided with her near the telephone booths and that she had seen him throw two of the bombs. The former police chief was sentenced to six months in the county jail in a jury trial, but on appeal, he was awarded a new hearing, where he pleaded guilty, paid a $100 fine and was paroled.

A bizarre incident in January 1950 sent a seventy-four-year-old woman to the hospital and damaged a limousine, a police car and a convertible. It could have been much worse. A giant slab of ice broke loose from the Roof Garden and became a missile as it plunged nine stories, slamming into three cars parked on Main Street. Rolena Carter, a retired Joplin teacher, had taken an American Airlines flight from Chicago to Joplin and then an airport limousine to the Connor. She was still seated inside when the ice fell; the vehicle's metal top saved her life, although she did go into shock.

Police Sergeant Clay Brown had been called to the hotel just minutes before, when employees had noticed the pending danger and requested barricades to keep pedestrians away. Brown had returned to his patrol car to report the situation just as the ice slammed through his windshield. "It sounded like a clap of thunder," he told the *Globe*. He ended up with a forty-pound chunk of ice in his lap, his pants cuffs and shoes full of glass and the legs of his pants nearly half cut off. "It was a new uniform, too." (The Connor later paid the city $201.15 for damages to the police car.)

At least two gangsters stopped at the Connor: Joe Palmer, a member of Clyde Barrow's gang, and Pretty Boy Floyd. Barrow himself dropped off Palmer at the hotel on January 29, 1934, just thirteen days after he and Bonnie Parker had freed him and four other inmates from the Eastham

Prison Farm in Texas. Palmer, an old friend of Barrow's, shot and killed a prison guard during the breakout.

Palmer registered at the Connor under the name "Joe Givens" but stayed for only one night. He left in a hurry the next day, failing to pay his bill and leaving a suitcase behind. The suitcase contained shoes, shirts, underwear, two detective magazines, some leather leggings and other miscellaneous items. After Bonnie and Clyde were killed on May 23, 1934, Palmer was captured three weeks later in St. Joseph, Missouri, and returned to Texas. The penitentiary sent a letter to the Connor soon after on Palmer's behalf, asking the hotel to return his suitcase. Manager J.A. Laws didn't ponder his response for long: Palmer could have his suitcase back when he paid his bill. The desperado never did get his items back—he was executed in the electric chair a year later.

Due to its reputation as a wide-open, unruly mining town, Joplin saw more than its fair share of criminals passing through. Charles Arthur "Pretty Boy" Floyd, who grew up 135 miles away in Akins, Oklahoma, spent plenty of time there in various bootlegging pursuits. He always felt safe in Joplin, even when he was on his way to becoming "Public Enemy No. 1." Ozarks folklorist Vance Randolph (1892–1980) claimed that he met Floyd once at the Connor Hotel.

"He used to come into towns like Joplin, and the police knew he was there, and everybody knew all about it, but they never bothered him," Randolph said in a 1977 interview. "He didn't do any robbing in Joplin, but he came in there." Randolph said a newspaperman tipped him off that Floyd would be at the Connor for an interview in half an hour and that he could sit in on it if he wanted to. "Pretty Boy liked to get his name in the paper, and these newspaper boys all knew him—all of them—and they strung along with him as best they could."

GEORGE WASHINGTON
SLEPT HERE

Despite the occasional rogue guest, the Connor normally boasted a much higher class of clientele. Nearly every celebrity who passed through town spent a night or two there. The list constitutes a who's who of the first half of the twentieth century. There were actors, athletes, musicians, politicians and even a giant who stood nearly nine feet tall. Harry Truman stayed there multiple times before becoming president, but during his first visit to Joplin, he couldn't even afford a night in Joplin's finest.

A struggling farmer in 1916, Truman, along with two others, invested in a lead and zinc mine at Commerce, Oklahoma, thirty miles southwest of Joplin. None of the three knew anything about mining, but they thought they could turn a tidy profit once the Eureka Mine's mill was repaired. Truman stayed periodically at the Yates Hotel in Joplin, meeting with a mill expert, buying supplies and looking at machinery to purchase. "Some day I hope to be able to quit buying and go to selling," he wrote his wife-to-be, Bess, from the hotel. Staying at the Connor was a luxury he could not afford.

When Truman returned to Joplin eight years later, for the state American Legion convention, he took a room at the Connor. His fortunes had improved; he was the eastern judge of Jackson County, although he would lose his bid for reelection in three months.

As a newly elected U.S. senator, Truman spent the night at the Connor again in September 1935 on his way to a speaking engagement in Muskogee, Oklahoma. He hosted a dinner at the hotel for a small group of Joplin

Harry Truman used Hotel Connor stationery to write this letter to wife Bess on August 18, 1924. *Harry S. Truman Library.*

residents, most likely his Democratic supporters. He spent a few hours at the Connor in June 1940, before speaking at the Truman-for-Senator headquarters at 312 Main—three doors north of the hotel—as part of his reelection campaign. He had been expected to spend the night at the Connor following his 8:00 p.m. address but left by train for St. Louis afterward.

Truman spoke from the rooftop of the Connor in October 1942, in support of the Missouri Democratic ticket for the upcoming election. An informal reception at the hotel and a band concert in front of it preceded his address, which was broadcast by WMBH radio. Truman advocated the defeat of southwest Missouri's beloved congressman, Republican Dewey Short. "He has not supported the defense program and he has not given proper support to the war effort," Truman said.

According to the *St. Louis Star and Times*, Truman spent a "hectic 24 hours at the Connor Hotel" on August 30–31, 1944, just before formally accepting the Democratic Party's vice presidential nomination in Lamar, Missouri, his birthplace. Truman arrived at the hotel by automobile from Kansas City at 1:45 p.m. on Wednesday afternoon and was welcomed by a cheering reception committee in the lobby. He then went to Camp Crowder at the invitation of Major General Walter E. Prosser for a tour and dinner, returning to the Connor shortly before 8:00 p.m. His day wasn't over, however; the Joplin Democratic Women's Club held a reception in his honor.

Ten Democratic U.S. senators—the party's official notification committee—arrived by train at 6:30 a.m. the next morning and were taken to the Connor by a local reception committee: Tom Connally of Texas (chairman of the Senate Foreign Relations Committee), Joseph Guffey of Pennsylvania, Carl Hatch of New Mexico, John McClellan of Arkansas, Ernest MacFarland of Arizona, James Mead of New York, Abe Murdock of Utah, Claude Pepper of Florida (who would oppose Truman's presidential nomination in 1948), Elmer Thomas of Oklahoma and David Worth Clark of Idaho. Truman met them for breakfast and a press conference at the hotel three hours later. He didn't leave for Lamar until after he had lunch with Frank and Juanita Wallower at their Mission Hills Farm, now the home to Missouri Southern State University.

Truman didn't arrive in Lamar until 4:00 p.m., two or three hours later than expected. City officials were "hopping mad," feeling that Joplin had upstaged them on the biggest day in their town's history. Joplin, thirty-five miles south, had been asked to provide accommodations, entertainment and transportation for the hundreds of politicians, newspapermen, radio

Senator Harry S Truman has breakfast at the Connor Hotel with Senator Tom Connally (*left*) and Senator Carl Hatch (*right*) on August 31, 1944. *Harry S. Truman Library.*

announcers, newsreel representatives and out-of-town guests but held on to Roosevelt's third running mate perhaps a bit longer than necessary.

Three sitting vice presidents also visited the Connor: James "Sunny Jim" Sherman in 1910, Thomas Marshall in 1916 and Alben Barkley in 1950. None spent the night.

Sherman, who ran on the 1908 Republican ticket with William Howard Taft, arrived at 8:10 a.m. one late August morning on a Frisco train from Springfield. He was driven the three blocks from the depot at Sixth and Virginia to the Connor by *Joplin Globe* owner Alfred H. Rogers. Following a brief reception in the hotel lobby, Sherman had breakfast in the banquet room on the second floor with a group of twenty supporters that included Rogers and Mayor Guy Humes. Leaving the hotel wasn't quite as easy; Sherman had to wade through the packed lobby and shake hundreds of hands before departing in Rogers's car for a tour of the mining district. He gave speeches in Prosperity, Webb City, Carthage and back in Joplin at the Club Theater.

Marshall, who ran on the 1912 and 1916 tickets with Woodrow Wilson, attracted a crowd of five thousand when he spoke from a big tent at Fifth and Byers on the afternoon of September 12, 1916—the beginning of the Democratic campaign in Missouri. Marshall, his wife and U.S. Speaker of the House Champ Clark arrived at the Frisco depot at 9:00 a.m. to a brass band and a cheering crowd of five hundred. They were driven to the Connor, where they were joined by U.S. Senator James Reed and Congressman Perl Decker for an "old-fashioned, hand-shaking event."

Barkley, who ran on the 1948 ticket with Truman, was greeted by more than five hundred supporters at the Joplin Municipal Airport on an October Saturday afternoon. A motor caravan with a police escort took the vice president to Twentieth and Main for a parade with bands and drum corps down Main Street. The "fine Kentucky gentleman of the old school" got out at the Connor to review the procession from the east front door. Afterward, Barkley held a press conference at the hotel and then spoke to a crowd of two thousand in Memorial Hall.

A vice presidential nominee arrived at the Joplin Municipal Airport on October 21, 1952—exactly two weeks before the presidential election. Richard and Pat Nixon were taken by a motor caravan to the Connor, where they had dinner and a rest before heading to Memorial Hall. Running short of attire on the grueling campaign trail, Pat Nixon managed to slip away from the hotel to buy two dresses at Richards' ready-to-wear store, which reopened for her.

Ronald Reagan, then a movie and television star, came to Joplin on May 8, 1958, as the keynote speaker for the chamber of commerce's annual banquet. About two hundred people attended a cocktail party in his honor at the Joplin Club in the Connor before the banquet at Memorial Hall that attracted twice as many. Reagan, who spoke on "The Business in Show Business," spent the night in Parsons, Kansas.

Eleanor Roosevelt's visit on Sunday, October 16, 1938, was the first time a president's wife ever set foot in the city. She came to speak on "Peace" as part of Mrs. Jay L. Wilder's Joplin Town Hall and All-Star Concert Series program. Four hundred people gathered at the Frisco station to greet her special Pullman coach, which arrived at 12:42 p.m. The first lady went directly to the Connor, where the master suite had been specially prepared for her.

Roosevelt read several letters that had been sent to her at the hotel and then conducted an informal press conference in her suite at one o'clock. Only women were allowed at her news conferences, a tradition she started

Eleanor Roosevelt in her suite at the Connor on October 16, 1938. *Joplin Historical &*
Mineral Museum.

only two days after becoming first lady in 1933. One of the reporters was
sixteen-year-old Hildred Bebee, a junior at Joplin High School and member
of the *Spyglass* newspaper staff. Roosevelt, perhaps sensing that Bebee was
"practically petrified," insisted that the girl sit on the couch next to her. At
the end of the questions, Roosevelt warmly shook her hand and said, "I wish
you all the luck in the world in your chosen profession."

Roosevelt's 3:30 p.m. speech at Memorial Hall drew an audience of
nearly two thousand. Attendees paid $2.50 per ticket to sit on the first ten
rows, $2.00 to sit elsewhere in the auditorium or in the first three rows of
the balcony or $1.50 to sit in the back rows of the balcony. An eighty-piece
ROTC band from Joplin High School, directed by T. Frank Coulter, gave
a half-hour concert before her presentation. Afterward, in an informal
reception backstage, she personally thanked all of the band members.

The first lady then returned to her suite at the Connor and stayed there
until shortly before her train departed at 9:15 p.m. that evening. Although
only a few persons were present to see her off, the JHS students weren't the

only ones left with a good impression. The *Globe* editorialized that she had a "pleasing stage presence" and spoke with "clarity and forcefulness."

Ferne Wilder, who was always known as Mrs. Jay L. Wilder (her husband was a pharmacist), brought more than 250 cultural events to Joplin between 1933 and 1962. The list included violinists, cellists, pianists, vocalists, opera companies, choruses, musical comedy acts, orchestras and bands, theater companies, children's theater, dancers, guest speakers and travelogues. Wilder sold tickets from her office in the Connor annex lobby, and the majority of the performers and speakers stayed at the hotel.

The guest speakers included Admiral Richard Byrd, Dale Carnegie, Edgar A. Guest, Sinclair Lewis and Drew Pearson. Byrd, who claimed to be the first person to fly over the North Pole and the South Pole, gave matinee and evening presentations at Memorial Hall on October 27, 1936. When the famous explorer arrived at the Connor at 10:30 a.m. that Tuesday morning, he was surprised to be greeted by two companies of Sea

John Carter (*right*), the young tenor of the Metropolitan Opera, and his accompanist, James Quillian, share a moment with Ferne Wilder at the Connor Hotel in January 1940. *Joplin Historical & Mineral Museum.*

Scouts saluting him from each side of Main Street. Byrd stood at attention as an ROTC band played the "General's March," featuring a flourish of trumpets and a ruffle of drums.

Season tickets for the four or five Joplin Town Hall lectures on late Sunday afternoons were limited to four hundred people due to the seating capacity of the Connor rooftop. Following a short question-and-answer session, patrons could stay for a Sunday evening buffet supper for an additional charge and informally meet the speakers. When Carnegie came to town on March 27, 1938, Wilder moved his presentation to the Joplin High School auditorium to accommodate all the businesses that purchased blocks of tickets for their employees. The "celebrity supper" that followed was held in the Empire Ballroom rather than on the roof.

Wilder, who got to know many of the visiting celebrities on a personal level, was particularly moved by Guest, the "People's Poet." He was the ideal speaker for a Joplin audience; the *Globe* had published more than seven thousand of his poems—one in every issue since March 26, 1918. There was only one problem: Guest had failed as a public speaker years before and was reluctant to come. Wilder convinced him, however, and even helped him put together a lecture tour that included stops in Milwaukee, Dallas, San Antonio, Austin and Kansas City.

But upon his arrival in Joplin on November 9, 1940, Guest apologized to Wilder and told her that she had made a big mistake in booking him. A huge crowd packed the Connor roof the following afternoon to hear him recite poems and describe his trials of working in a drugstore as a youth and trying to grow roses in the yellow clay of his Detroit backyard. "There were many moist eyes in his audience that afternoon as he read and interpreted poems and discussed his thoughts about living," the *Globe* recalled when Guest died in 1959. "Yet, still oblivious to the fact that he had spellbound his listeners, he wrote on an autographed photograph for Mrs. Wilder as he departed: 'From Your Never-Should-Have-Come Friend.'" Wilder, for her part, described him as "the most sincerely modest man I ever met."

Pearson, the "most widely read, most listened to journalist in America" for three decades, spoke on the Connor roof and participated in a "celebrity supper" on March 31, 1940. He coauthored a syndicated column called "Washington Merry-Go-Round" that was carried by nearly a thousand newspapers—including the *Globe*—and had millions of readers.

Singer and actor Nelson Eddy was Wilder's favorite performer. She brought him to Joplin three times (1935, 1937 and 1949) as part of her All-Star Concert Series and to Springfield in 1936. His 1935 movie

Naughty Marietta, co-starring Jeanette MacDonald and produced by Metro-Goldwyn-Mayer, had just been released by the time of his first Joplin visit, on April 3. A Hollywood columnist declared a month before his appearance, "[T]all and handsome Nelson Eddy takes his place with the leading luminaries of filmdom." That Wilder had booked Eddy nearly a year earlier was a real coup.

It's no surprise that he received numerous demands for encores during his concert at the Fox Theater. He also showed off a lighter side during a pre-conference interview in the Connor lobby. When a Connor Beverage Store employee came through wheeling a cart full of fancy liquors, Eddy took off in mock pursuit and stopped just short of pilfering a bottle—much to the disappointment of the audience that had gathered to observe his interview.

Eddy's star power had increased exponentially by the time he returned to Joplin two years later. He had been voted the Best Male Singer in a *Modern Screen Magazine* poll, he was receiving thousands of letters each day from his film and radio admirers and he and MacDonald had just released their third musical, *Maytime*. Eddy came to Joplin from Detroit, where he had drawn an audience of six thousand. The *Globe* noted that this would be the smallest city he would perform in this year.

Wilder, though, was worried about Eddy's health and ability to sing. He was on a five-month coast-to-coast tour, making forty-four appearances in twenty-eight states, and had been suffering from head colds, a streptococcus infection of the throat and sinus attacks. Relieved to see him arrive at the Frisco station the morning of his concert, she gave him strict instructions to take it easy in his suite at the Connor. A crowd grew in the lobby as he rested, waiting for him to make an appearance. He did give an interview to a *News Herald* reporter, who noted that he appeared to be in excellent health while smoking several cigarettes. When a near-capacity audience in Memorial Hall gave him ten encores that evening, no one was more pleased than Wilder.

MacDonald, Eddy's equally famous co-star in eight motion pictures, came to Joplin herself in June 1943. Wilder picked up the "First Lady of Song," her concert manager and his assistant, her accompanist, her personal manager and her personal maid at the Neosho rail station and took them to the Connor. MacDonald spent three days at the hotel, using the time to rehearse with her accompanist and getting some much-needed rest. She did visit a Red Cross surgical dressing class at Memorial Hall and spent an hour folding bandages to send to hospitals overseas.

Main Street, Joplin, Missouri

The Hotel Connor as it appeared on Main Street in 1943. *Joplin Historical Postcards/Joplin Public Library.*

The standing room–only crowd of more than three thousand in Memorial Hall included Camp Crowder officers, soldiers and two hundred members of the Women's Army Auxiliary Corps. MacDonald opened the program by singing the national anthem and inviting the audience to join in. Despite an unusually warm evening in early June, the perspiring concertgoers were not dissuaded from demanding encore after encore.

By the time Eddy returned to Joplin for the third time, his movie career was over. Once the top concert artist in the United States, he hadn't gone on tour in four years. Wilder was able to secure a spot on his 1949 nine-week tour, which didn't have room for fifty cities that wanted to be included.

From his suite in the Connor, Eddy gave a lengthy interview to a *News Herald* reporter. "It's not the size of the city that counts," he said. "It's the quality of the audience that counts. I haven't been here for 12 years, but if the audience is anything like it was then, it'll be a good one to play before." He had just come from Omaha, where he performed for a too-large audience of 9,300. "I had to use a mic," he lamented, "and when you use a mic you're not yourself." Eddy also told Wilder that he particularly liked the Memorial Hall stage. "The extended stage arrangements put the artist in closer touch with his audience and brings out the best he has to offer," he said.

Eddy's final Joplin concert had ten encores, including "Oh, What a Beautiful Mornin'" and his signature "Shortnin' Bread," which would be on any list today of politically incorrect songs. He signed concert programs for thirty minutes afterward, seemingly in no hurry to leave.

Lawrence Tibbett was at least Eddy's equal as a national celebrity. The leading baritone of the Metropolitan Opera in New York, Tibbett was also an international recording artist and a Hollywood star. He had even been nominated for Best Actor at the 1930 Academy Awards. Wilder brought him to Joplin in 1934 and 1939 for concerts in Memorial Hall.

For his first visit, Wilder had a piano installed in Tibbett's suite at the Connor so he could practice in the afternoon. He delighted the large audience with a wide selection of songs, including "Shortnin' Bread" and "Standin' in the Need of Prayer" from *The Emperor Jones*, an opera that had premiered at the Metropolitan Opera the year before.

Wilder became such a good friend of Tibbett's that he invited her to one of his famous New Year's Eve parties at the New York apartment he shared with his second wife, Jane. According to the opera star's biography, "The guest list for these gala events was so sparkling that they were always fully covered by the media." Wilder attended his 1937 party, where she urged him to make a return visit to Joplin.

Tibbett honored her request in February 1939, performing to an audience of 2,800 in Memorial Hall. The baritone stayed in a suite of several rooms at the Connor, where he granted an interview to reporters soon after arriving and having breakfast. The reporters seemed more interested in his voracious appetite rather than his musical abilities, noting that he had consumed a big steak for breakfast and normally ate a "flock of lamb chops" for lunch.

Numerous other celebrities who were not brought to Joplin by Wilder stayed or stopped at the Connor. They included Gene Autry, Ethel Barrymore, Constance Bennett, Joan Crawford, Walter Cronkite, Bette Davis, Peter Lawford, George "Spanky" McFarland and Robert Wadlow, the world's tallest man.

Autry, the "Singing Cowboy," flew his own plane to Joplin for his matinee and evening performances in Memorial Hall on January 17, 1949. His troupe of forty-five—which included sidekick Pat Buttram (who later played Mr. Haney on *Green Acres*); comedian Rufe Davis; the Pinafores vocal trio; the Cass County Boys music group; assorted cowboys; his horse, Champion; and a pony named Little Champion—arrived separately. Autry gave a show for the children at 4:15 p.m. and a standing room–only performance at 8:30 p.m. He also visited the Joplin Children's Home, wearing his ten-gallon hat and leading about fifty children in singing "Home on the Range."

The Connor was the scene of a romantic rendezvous between two Hollywood movie stars during the summer of 1942. Largely forgotten today, Constance Bennett had been one of the highest-paid stars of the early 1930s, reportedly earning $30,000 per week. Her fourth husband, the Mexican-born actor Gilbert Roland, who had only recently become a U.S. citizen, arrived at Camp Crowder on July 1 to receive his basic training. The private managed to secure a long weekend leave pass just a month later, and Bennett flew in to Kansas City and took a train to Joplin in order to meet him at the hotel.

Joan Crawford spent the night of April 16, 1957, at the Connor, not as an actress but as the wife of Alfred Steele, CEO of Pepsi-Cola. The Steeles were in town to open a new bottling plant at 501 Tyler Avenue. Crawford sent a letter to hotel manager Steve Howard a week later, thanking him for providing fruit and a daisy and chrysanthemum flower arrangement.

A capacity crowd in the Empire Room of the Connor heard Walter Cronkite speak on October 21, 1948. Invited by the Joplin Rotary Club, the thirty-one-year-old Cronkite had been serving as manager of the United Press bureau in Moscow. He shocked his audience by telling them that the Soviet capital was "one vast slum" and that as many as fifty people were forced to share a single bathroom. "You can't get over to them that an American factory worker owns a five-room house with a bathroom and a kitchen," he said.

Two-time Academy Award winner Bette Davis appeared in Memorial Hall on Sunday afternoon, September 13, 1942, as part of a war bonds show that also featured soldiers from Camp Crowder. Davis spent Saturday night at the Connor after giving talks in St. Joseph and Sedalia earlier in the day. She surprised bellboy Paul Ash with a twenty-five-dollar tip—a hundred times the size of his normal gratuity. The war bonds show drew a capacity crowd to Memorial Hall.

Actor Peter Lawford, who would go on to marry John F. Kennedy's younger sister, Patricia, and become a member of Frank Sinatra's "Rat Pack," spent the night of November 28, 1949, at the Connor. Lawford and his pal Peter Sabiston, a future film literary agent, were driving back to Hollywood from the Notre Dame–University of Southern California football game in South Bend, Indiana, when they figured Joplin was a good place to stop. They went to a movie, *Oh, You Beautiful Doll*, at the Paramount, where Lawford was recognized and forced to confront a mob of "autograph hounds" upon leaving the theater.

The youngest celebrity to stay at the Connor was nine-year-old George "Spanky" McFarland of *Our Gang* and *The Little Rascals* fame. George; his seven-year-old brother, Tommy; and their parents, Robert and Virginia, spent the night of March 11, 1938, en route from Hollywood to Hartford, Connecticut. The family was accompanied by Jack Pepper, a singer/comedian who was going to create a vaudeville act with George on the East Coast. "He has an awfully cute act," his mother told a *News Herald* reporter as the boys romped about the hotel lobby. "He has learned to play the trumpet, and he sings and talks with Mr. Pepper."

The world's tallest man, his father and his manager spent the nights of June 8–9, 1940, at the Connor while on a tour of Missouri, Kansas, Oklahoma and Arkansas for a St. Louis shoe company. Robert Wadlow, who was eight feet, eleven inches tall and wore size thirty-seven shoes, traveled in a specially made seven-passenger automobile. In an interview with a *Globe* reporter, he revealed that his hobbies were photography and collecting matchbooks and that he had planned on becoming a lawyer but gave it up for "a chance to travel at a substantial salary."

Sadly, Wadlow died not long after leaving Joplin at the age of twenty-two. He wore special braces on his legs but failed to notice that one was rubbing on his left ankle. An infected blister led to emergency surgery and a blood transfusion in Michigan. The "Gentle Giant," who had a weakened immune system, died in his sleep on July 15.

Numerous sports celebrities stopped at the Connor on visits to Joplin. Boxer Jack Dempsey stayed there at least three times. The "Manassa Mauler" had lunch at the hotel and checked into a suite a day before knocking out a Kansas City opponent in only seventy-five seconds at Miners Park on the Fourth of July in 1918. Exactly one year later, in Toledo, Ohio, Dempsey pummeled Jess Willard to become the new heavyweight champion of the world.

Dempsey returned in 1930, his seven-year reign as champion over but his stardom was greater than ever. Five hundred fans greeted him at the Frisco Depot, some following him to his suite (room 419) at the Connor and even managing to gain entrance to his room. His admirers watched as a barber was hastily summoned to shave the former boxer, but they did leave when it was time for Dempsey to take a bath. It would be his only time alone during his twelve-hour visit.

Dempsey spoke to an invited luncheon crowd of fifty at the Connor that included St. Louis Cardinals manager Gabby Street and many of the city's leading citizens. The fighter then visited patients at Freeman Hospital and St. John's Hospital, distributed candy at the Children's Home and Hospital, signed hundreds of autographs back at the hotel, conducted an interview on WMBH and then officiated at an American Legion fight card at Memorial Hall.

The largest crowd ever to witness a sporting event in Memorial Hall turned out four years later to see Dempsey referee a wrestling match. A crowd of three thousand filled every seat and overflowed into the aisles. Promoters even added several rows of bleachers onto the stage, but at least five hundred fans were turned away. Dempsey played to the crowd, twice cocking his fist as if he were going to deliver an uppercut to one of the contestants. He did manage to smack one of the wrestlers in the chin with a forearm.

St. Louis Cardinals pitchers Dizzy and Paul Dean spent a few hours at the Connor on October 5, 1935, as part of a barnstorming tour of all-star players. When their game against the Kansas City Monarchs was canceled due to cold weather and drizzle, the brothers amused themselves with a sack of torpedo firecrackers in the hotel lobby. "They were shooting them at people's feet in the lobby," recalled Joplin businessman Jack Parker, who was eleven at the time. "They had people dancing all over the place. They were having a ball."

The year 1935 was a banner one for sports celebrities stopping at the Connor, largely because of the city's location on Route 66. Kenesaw Mountain Landis, the commissioner of baseball, and his wife spent the night of April 3 as they were driving to Chicago for the season opener after spending three months in Arizona. Ellsworth Vines, the no. 1 tennis player in the world, and his wife lodged there on May 2 en route from Louisville to their home in Los Angeles. Walter Hagen, one of the greatest and most flamboyant golfers of all time, arrived at the Connor at 4:00 a.m. on October 15 in his cream-colored, 120-mile-per-hour Auburn supercharged speedster. He slept but four hours before leaving to play in a GPA tournament in Oklahoma City.

Several members of the St. Louis Cardinals came to Joplin in January 1950 to honor Gabby Street, their former World Series manager and current radio color commentator. Street had lived in the city since 1923, when he managed the Joplin Miners. The St. Louis contingent included Stan Musial, Red Schoendienst, Joe Garagiola, Enos "Country" Slaughter, Harry Caray and owner Fred Saigh.

Most of the group arrived at the Frisco Station on a Pullman, but Musial drove himself from Florida, pulling up to the Connor shortly after 1:00 a.m. The twenty-nine-year-old slugger left word at the front desk that he was not to be disturbed until nine o'clock the next morning. Musial, however, had parked his brand-new blue Cadillac in a bus loading zone at Fourth and Main, forcing city buses to load and unload passengers in the middle of Main Street throughout the morning.

Noticing all the Cardinals stickers on the Caddy, police finally figured out that it belonged to Stan the Man. A traffic sergeant named Bill Potts went to his room, which by now was full of the other players. Potts decided to play a joke, claiming that the car was being towed off due to the disruption of downtown traffic. As the group howled with laughter, Potts offered to call off the wrecker if Musial would surrender the keys. He gladly did, and the sergeant moved the car to a nearby garage. Showing Joplin's hospitality, Potts tore up the parking ticket when he returned the keys.

BEGINNING OF THE END

After twenty-three years of owning the Connor, Barney Allis had lost interest in the Joplin hostelry. He planned to enlarge his Hotel Muehlebach in Kansas City from 450 to 1,000 rooms and needed an infusion of capital. The $4 million project would add a twenty-seven-story tower and a 1,200-seat restaurant, making it one of the largest dining rooms in the country.

Allis began looking for a buyer in the fall of 1945, working with a Wichita real estate brokerage firm. Joplin residents could have taken a clue that a sale was imminent when Connor manager Charles Allis, Barney's younger brother, transferred to the Muehlebach in November. On the evening of March 5, 1946, he announced that he had sold the Connor annex and the lease on the original hotel to Alsonett Hotels. The purchase price was not disclosed but was thought to be about $1.2 million—the valuation of the annex, lease, furnishings, equipment and all other assets.

Alsonett Hotels, with headquarters in Tulsa, owned fifteen other hotels in Oklahoma, Texas, Louisiana, Florida and Indiana. The company was headed by President Charles H. Alberding and Vice-President Donald L. Connett, who combined their surnames to form the name. There is no explanation of where the *s* came from or why Alsonett had only one *n*.

He may not have realized it at the time, but in selling the Connor to Alsonett, Allis essentially signed the death certificate for the hotel. And per his custom of never entering a hotel once he had sold it, he never set foot in the Connor again.

The Connor Hotel in the early 1940s, shortly before it began to decline with the sale to Alsonett Hotels. *Joplin Historical & Mineral Museum.*

Alberding and Connett issued the following statement upon purchasing the hotel: "No changes in the operating staff and personnel are contemplated and it is planned to continue to operate the hotel under the highest possible standards. Some major improvements, supplementing those made within the past two years, are being considered. It is also planned to continue a major program of repairs, rehabilitation and decoration."

All three statements turned out to be bald-faced lies.

Alberding earlier had been chief of the foreign operations department for the Chicago-based Universal Oil Products Company and had also worked for the Petroleum Administration for War as director of refining during World War II. He spent a considerable amount of time in hotels during his career as a petroleum engineer, and that spurred his interest in operating them. He met Connett when he purchased four apartment hotels in Tulsa, and the two soon formed a partnership.

They started snatching up various properties in the early 1940s, starting with the Aldridge hotels in Shawnee and Ada, Oklahoma; the Goodhue and the Sabine in Port Arthur, Texas; the Grim in Texarkana, Texas; the Charleston in Lake Charles, Louisiana; the Coral Sands in Fort Lauderdale, Florida; and four resort hotels in the St. Petersburg, Florida area. The Connor became Alsonett's sixteenth property.

By 1959, Alsonett owned fifty hotels and motels totaling some 8,000 rooms and eight thousand employees. Its properties included the 250-room King Cotton Hotel in Memphis, purchased for excess of $1 million in 1948; the 625-room Peabody Hotel in Memphis, purchased for $7.495 million in 1953; and the 250-room Hermitage Hotel in Nashville, purchased for $2 million in 1956. Closer to Joplin, Alsonett also bought the 100-room Hotel Miami in Oklahoma for $350,000 in 1956.

Alberding's business strategy was to buy aging properties for as little as possible, invest next to nothing in improvements or renovations, squeeze out the maximum amount of profit and close them rather than sell them. He would let his hotels depreciate to the point where they had no tax basis left, claimed the *Tampa Bay Times* in 1989. "To sell them would have meant paying federal government taxes on the profit."

Alsonett had purchased the elegant waterfront hotel, the Vinoy Park, in nearby St. Petersburg in 1945. The Vinoy was allowed to deteriorate to the point where it had to close thirty years later. "In North Redington Beach, Tallahassee and San Diego, Alberding is equally unpopular," a reporter for the *St. Petersburg Times* wrote in 1982. "Officials in those cities cite fire hazards, rat infestations, peeling paint and dingy wallpaper, among other things, when they accuse Alberding of being an irresponsible, cheapskate landlord."

Other cities where Alberding owned hotels told similar stories. In Memphis, Alsonett's ownership of the famous Peabody, the "South's Grand Hotel," lasted only twelve years. "Alsonett set aside tradition in favor of economy," noted the

Historic Memphis website. "Cost cutting practices were evident everywhere. Downgrading was the name of the game. And any profits were used to upgrade Alsonett properties elsewhere. The profitable convention business completely disappeared. The hotel faced huge debts and was unable to get financing. In 1965, the grand old Peabody was forced into foreclosure."

In Nashville, "after years of difficulty and deterioration," Alsonett closed the Hermitage after twenty-three years of ownership. In Wilson, North Carolina, the city condemned the chain's Cherry Hotel in 1981 after finding rats, pigeons and vagrants inside and the windows leading to the fire escapes nailed shut. The hotel also lacked a sprinkler system.

Alberding made the national news in 1961 when the New York Yankees and the St. Louis Cardinals requested that his Soreno and Vinoy hotels in St. Petersburg end segregation and allow black players to stay there during spring training. It all started when the president of the local NAACP chapter told reporters that he would no longer find private homes for the Yankees' black players. Yankees co-owner Dan Topping agreed that it was time for the Soreno to house the entire team—including World Series hero Elston Howard—"under one roof." The Cardinals made a similar request of the Vinoy.

Alberding wouldn't budge, though, and issued the following statement on February 2, 1961: "We've been happy to entertain the Yankees at the Soreno and we'll be happy to continue on the same basis. At the Vinoy Park, we are happy to entertain the Cardinals as per our original agreement. But when either the Yankees or the Cardinals, or both, feel the situation has developed so they must insist on housing all their personnel in the same hotel, then the Yankees and the Cardinals should look for other hotels."

Both teams did exactly that. The Yankees moved their spring training camp to Fort Lauderdale, and the Cardinals took over a large motel near Tampa Bay that could also accommodate the players' wives and children.

Alberding had encountered strife in Joplin when about 60 of the Connor's 160 employees went on strike and formed picket lines in 1951 after several workers had been fired. The strike was organized by the local Hotel and Restaurant Employees and Bartenders' International Union, which sought a working contract that included higher wages, insurance and sick leave. Hotel manager Harry Nash said the Connor didn't enter into contracts with employees but provided many benefits, including vacations.

The strikers included clerks, maids, dishwashers, busboys, waitresses, laundry workers, doormen, elevator operators, cashiers and porters. The picket lines operated eighteen hours a day and surrounded the hotel—on

Main Street, Fourth Street, Joplin Avenue and an alley at the rear. Deliveries by companies employing union workers came to a complete halt.

After a month, the striking workers returned to their jobs. There had been no settlement, and the union made no announcement. It can be assumed that the employees couldn't hold out any longer due to the continued loss of their wages.

Despite the turmoil, business continued to boom at the Connor. The hotel inaugurated a catering service in 1951, delivering food and drink for receptions, showers, banquets, industrial parties and luncheons. For weddings, it advertised that it furnished "Everything but the Bride."

Connor manager Judd Sampson reported in 1953 that 81,202 guests stayed at the hotel the year before—an average of 222 per night. Several clubs were also meeting regularly there, including the Rotary, Kiwanis, Lions, Explorers, Sertoma and Soroptimist clubs.

The Alsonett chain made the necessary basic repairs to keep the Connor operating but invested next to nothing in improvements or renovations. The only project undertaken during its ownership was a redecoration of the Kit Kat and Rendezvous and a reupholstering of the restaurants' furniture in 1954.

The U.S. Air Force rented the Connor's rooftop in August 1955 for an Air Defense Filter Center, one of only sixty-seven in the country. Designed to prevent the bombing of American cities by the Soviets, the centers were staffed by civilian volunteers who took reports from field observers and notified direction centers of potential enemy aircraft. The Joplin center opened on February 1, 1956, and closed three years later when vast improvements in the country's radar networks and the creation of the Distant Early Warning (DEW) Line above the Arctic Circle made the filter centers obsolete.

A 1958 prostitution incident at the Connor illustrated how far the hotel had fallen. A thirty-three-year-old woman claimed that her forty-nine-year-old husband had forced her to meet men in the bar and charge them fifteen or twenty dollars to accompany them to their room. She even said the hotel's bellhops had been instructed to call her if someone was interested in her services. In return, she would split the proceeds with them. She went on these "dates," she said, to support the couple and their eleven-year-old son and eight-year-old daughter.

The world's oldest profession or the indifference of the Alsonett chain weren't the greatest threats to the well-being of Connor, however. Something far more ominous was occurring four miles southeast of the hotel: the beginning of Range Line Road's motel district.

Even before President Dwight Eisenhower signed a bill in 1956 to create the Interstate Highway System, Joplin already was known as the "Crossroads of America." While a few other cities also laid claim to this distinction, Joplin could point to the fact that U.S. Highway 66 ("the Main Street of America") and U.S. Highway 71 (also known as the Jefferson Highway) intersected in the city at Seventh and Main. The Mother Road, in fact, ran right through the heart of downtown Joplin and past the Connor Hotel.

The 88.5-mile Will Rogers Turnpike from Tulsa to the Missouri state line opened on June 28, 1957. Six months earlier, the state highway department had completed a 9-mile, four-lane, divided "superhighway" from the state line to Range Line Road (Highways 71 and 166). This became the main entrance into Joplin from the west, which had huge ramifications for the Connor Hotel and the entire downtown district. There was a South Main Street exit from the freeway, but it was nearly five miles to Fourth and Main.

It's no surprise that developers started targeting Range Line, with its proximity to what would become Interstate 44 in a few years. Baxter Springs, Kansas highway contractor Harold Youngman and New York Yankees slugger Mickey Mantle bought a franchise and opened Mickey Mantle's Holiday Inn in October 1957. Mantle, who was from nearby Commerce, Oklahoma, and had played for the Joplin Miners, met Youngman during the 1952 off season and became fast friends with the former traveling salesman.

The fifty-three-room "motor hotel" at 2600 Range Line, which reportedly cost $500,000, offered these amenities:

- *Ample parking for guests at their front door*
- *Bellhop and porter service*
- *Year-round air conditioning with individual controls to dial your own weather*
- *Local and long-distance telephone in every room, with a switchboard operator on duty 24 hours a day*
- *"Triple play" system of radio, 21-inch television, and background music in every room*
- *Large swimming pool with a shallow end for the children, and a wading pool*
- *Glamorous poolside dining and lounging*
- *Cocktail lounge*
- *Valet service to freshen travel-weary clothes*

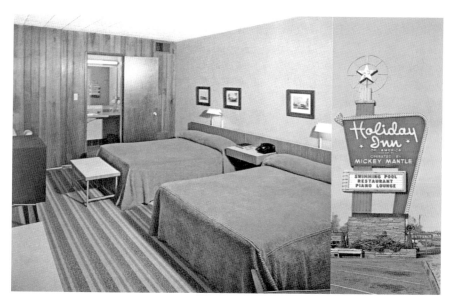

The opening of Mickey Mantle's Holiday Inn in Joplin in October 1957 signaled the beginning of the end for the Connor Hotel. *Joplin Historical Postcards/Joplin Public Library.*

- *Restaurant and adjoining 150-seat banquet room*
- *Complete food and beverage room service*
- *Automatic icemakers only a few steps away*
- *Bonded babysitters*
- *House physicians*

Mantle and Youngman added another fifty guest rooms in December 1958 and "The Dugout" in February 1959. Billed as the "district's most unusual cocktail lounge," it resembled a baseball dugout complete with green carpeting, sky-blue walls, a mural depicting the New York skyline, a huge picture of Yankee Stadium and baseball pennants on the walls.

Other motels soon came to Range Line, courtesy of Fred B. Van Pelt (father) and Fred L. Van Pelt (son). They built the twenty-room Rocket Motel for an estimated $57,500 in late 1957 at 1001 Range Line. They sold it one year later for a reported sum in excess of $150,000, using the profits to help construct the thirty-unit Thunderbird Motel at 2121 Range Line. The Thunderbird, which boasted a swimming pool and living quarters for the owner, welcomed its first guests in November 1958.

Meanwhile, Range Line was being widened to four lanes to connect to the "superhighway" that had been built just to the south to meet up with the interstate highway. The $2 million project started just south of the Jasper-Newton county line and extended 6.5 miles north to Webb City, where it connected with Highways 71 and 66.

The sixty-one-unit Sands Motor Lodge at 1600 Range Line opened in April 1959. The $425,000 motel boasted a ninety-thousand-gallon heated swimming pool, a restaurant with a seating capacity of 170, coffee shop, cocktail lounge, banquet rooms and twenty-four-hour switchboard service. Many of the city's civic organizations also started having their meetings there, including the South Joplin Lions Club, the Joplin Toastmasters Club and the Tri-State Salesmen's Club.

Mickey Mantle's took even more meeting business away from the Connor. The Exchange Club, the Sertoma Club, the Soroptimist Club, the Joplin chapter of the American Business Women's Association, the Newcomers Club, the Joplin Shriners and the Last Man's Club of World War I were among the groups having luncheons or dinner meetings at the Holiday Inn.

The *Globe* seemed more concerned about the Connor's plight than Alsonett officials. Rex Newman, editor of the editorial page, wrote on July 5, 1959, that the hotel had been "menaced by the luxury hotel building program, the same as outlying shopping centers hit downtown shops and department stores." Newman had a front-row seat to what was happening—his office was a block away from the hotel.

The situation wasn't unique to the Connor Hotel and Joplin. Across the country, the number of hotel rooms was decreasing as the number of rooms in motor hotels and motels soared dramatically. "As more Americans traveled by automobile, the old downtown hotels designed to serve rail passengers seemed increasingly out of date and accounted for a diminishing share of the lodging business," wrote Jon C. Teaford in *The Metropolitan Revolution: The Rise of Post-Urban America.*

The Van Pelts opened the Riviera Motel at 3333 Range Line in February 1960. The 30-unit motel offered guests a large swimming pool and a free continental breakfast. Two years later, the family teamed up with Joplin's famous movie and TV star to open the 102-room Bob Cummings Motor Hotel. The hoteliers had a knack for choosing easy-to-remember addresses for their properties. The newest one, at 3535 Range Line, had an access road so that guests at the Riviera could use all the amenities at the Bob Cummings. These amenities included the Celebrity Room Supper Club, which could accommodate up to 250 people for dining and dancing; adjoining "Wilshire" and "Cinema" banquet rooms, which could hold an additional 200; the Studio Room, the main dining room that could seat 100; a twenty-four-hour coffee shop; and a swimming pool that resembled Cummings's own at his home in California.

As all these new motels thrived on Range Line, the half-century-old Connor in downtown Joplin struggled to survive. Unfortunately, things were only going to get worse.

WELL, HERE'S ANOTHER
FINE MESS THE CONNOR
HAS GOTTEN INTO

The Joplin branch of the American Association of University Women held a luncheon program titled "The Soaring Sixties" in the Empire Room of the Connor on January 16, 1960. The program title was a misnomer, as far as the hotel was concerned. The next ten years would turn out to be disastrous, culminating in the closing of the longtime Joplin landmark while it was entangled in a legal quagmire.

The decade started with the Connor Investment Company, which still owned the original, front half of the hotel while leasing it to the Alsonett Hotel Company, challenging its real estate valuation. The Jasper County Board of Equalization thought the property was worth much more than it actually was and assessed it at 85 percent of the perceived market value. The Connor Investment Company, consisting of some of Tom Connor's heirs, hired an experienced real estate appraiser and a tax attorney to argue its case. The board reduced its assessment to 75 percent of market value, which the heirs thought was still a "staggering and inequitable tax burden." The company was expecting a 30 percent assessment.

Ralph Nolan, Connor's great-nephew, then began negotiations with Alsonett to sell the 210 rooms that the investment company still owned. The deal was finalized on Christmas Eve 1960 for $275,000—about half the amount that Connor had spent fifty-four years earlier to build the hotel. "Our time has run out, and we have failed in our attempt to give Joplin a fine, refurbished hotel," Nolan said. "We had no choice but to sell. Such a

The Connor on August 13, 1960, during a downtown sidewalk bazaar that brought an estimated crowd of twenty-five thousand during the twelve-hour event. *Joplin Historical & Mineral Museum.*

recourse will prove beyond a doubt the true market value of the hotel—thereby providing a more realistic basis for the tax valuation."

Nolan said the heirs had planned to remodel the entire front portion of the hotel, including the Main Street exterior portion. "But we couldn't do anything until the tax was lowered to a fair and equitable basis," he told the *Globe.* "Last year, for instance, it took five months' rent [from Alsonett] to pay the property tax."

The *Globe* endorsed the sale to Alsonett, which took effect on May 1, 1961, saying it preserved the hotel while benefiting the downtown and the city as a whole. "A monument to the one-time mineral wealth of this district and to the vision of one of its rugged individualists, the Connor still provides Joplin with much of its metropolitan atmosphere, an anchor for the central business district."

Although it had lost a good chunk of its lodging business to the Range Line motels and suffered a noticeable depreciation, the Connor continued to command a presence. Nothing could compete with its Roof Garden, which still served as the prime meeting place for large gatherings. A concert featuring twenty-one-year-old Jimmy Clanton ("Just a Dream"), Frankie Ford ("Sea Cruise") and The Champs ("Tequila") rocked the ballroom on May 6, 1960.

Five hundred people packed the ninth floor on September 20, 1960, for a performance by Thomas L. Thomas, a popular baritone of stage, radio and television. On March 23, 1961, in celebration of Joplin's eighty-eighth birthday, 461 people viewed historical exhibits, heard presentations, met descendants of early settlers and sang popular songs from the late 1800s, including "There Is a Tavern in the Town."

The Connor's final brushes with grandeur came courtesy of two formal galas to benefit the George A. Spiva Center for the Arts. The first St. Avips (Spiva spelled backward) Ball took place on the evening of Tuesday, April 16, 1963, in the hotel's Empire Room and adjoining Joplin Club. The 220 guests participated in a "grand march," walking across a red carpet and up the stairway to the candlelit second floor, where each couple was announced by Russ Carlyle, a well-known dance orchestra conductor from New York. The second floor had been transformed into a formal garden terrace, complete with wrought-iron and silver candelabra, bronzed cherubs, a stone fountain and bouquets of white tulips and Japanese iris.

A year later, the Thirty Friends of St. Avips transformed the Roof Garden into a New Orleans courtyard for the second annual ball. "Massive wrought iron gates opened into the ballroom, which was bathed in the soft glow of tall French Quarter post lights and scores of rose-tinted hurricane lamps," the *Globe* reported. "Flanking the entrance on the right was a tulip garden with a small stone figure of Pan with his pipes. On the left was a grouping of pink iron garden furniture." The 220 guests danced to an eleven-piece orchestra, while a cocktail buffet was served throughout the evening.

At the end of 1964, the Connor's annual gross revenue had dropped to $247,000, with an average daily occupancy rate of only 21 percent. The hotel had grossed $1 million per year in its heyday. The plunge paralleled the decline in Joplin's convention business, from $1 million in 1963 to $467,000 in 1964.

To save the Connor would require the restoration and expansion of the city's one-time booming convention business. Alsonett and city officials had numerous discussions in the 1960s about construction of a convention center behind or just to the north of the Connor. That now had the backing of Pace '73, a community development action program organized by the Joplin Chamber of Commerce in 1963 to complete twelve major projects by the city's centennial in ten years. One of the projects was the "[d]evelopment of a convention center to help the city capture its potential in what has been described as an untapped industry for Joplin."

The city sought a pledge from Alsonett that it would remodel and renovate the hotel before it would build a multi-level convention center and parking structure at Third and Main, where the Connor currently had a parking lot. The structure would have three levels of parking and spaces for 275 cars—116 on the ground level, 81 on the second level and 78 on the third floor. A 3,500-seat convention center would be on the fourth floor, with runways connecting it to the hotel. There would also be a lobby, restrooms and dining/catering facilities. The Connor would have exclusive rights to the catering business in exchange for donating the land for the center.

Meanwhile, Alsonett had contracted with Burl Garvin, a Joplin real estate agent, to look for a buyer for the hotel. Garvin received several offers, both locally and out of state, but they were either too low or contingent on the addition of the adjoining convention center. Alsonett's insistence that the Connor was worth $1.22 million dissuaded several potential buyers.

Pace '73 members continued to press the hotel chain for a $300,000 renovation that would include new entrances to the main lobby, the Rendezvous cocktail lounge and the Fourth Street side; sandblasting and cleaning of the marble facing on the front of the building; complete remodeling of the lobby with new carpeting and furniture; major improvements to the Rendezvous and the coffee shop; and remodeling of three floors of rooms in the annex.

John Hazlett, manager of the Connor, dropped a bombshell on thirty-eight Joplin businessmen the day after April Fools' in 1965. Expecting to discuss the specifics of the remodeling and the convention center, the chamber of commerce representatives were floored when Hazlett told them that Alsonett could not afford to renovate the hotel but would be willing to sell it to them for $564,000 cash. The manager explained that the hotel was losing $4,500 per month and might have to close if it was not sold.

Some of the businessmen soon stepped up and agreed to buy the Connor, providing they could have an eighteen-month option to pull out. "We offered to buy the hotel for the cash price, but we needed the option period to have a feasibility study made concerning improvements needed at the hotel, and cost of a convention center and whether the voters of Joplin would approve a bond issue for such a center," Morgan Hillhouse, spokesman for the businessmen, told the *News Herald*. Alberding turned down the offer, leaving the future of the hotel and the convention center in limbo.

With no progress or even any movement nine months later, the *News Herald* took aim at Alsonett in an editorial, saying, "[B]y the policy of the owners to spend no—or virtually no—money on the aging hostelry that it will require the utmost in financial and inn-keeping wizardry if the Connor is ever again to operate on anything like the scale it once did."

A member of the board of trustees of the new Missouri Southern College suggested in April 1966 that the college obtain three or four floors of the hotel and offer housing to students at a special price during the 1966–67 academic year, until MSC moved to its new campus. While that didn't happen, the college did house its athletes at the hotel. The newly formed Lionbackers booster club paid for the rooms and one meal per day; the athletes had to pay for their other meals.

Joplin's urban renewal program got into the act, commissioning a feasibility/engineering study on the Connor in 1966. The preliminary report by the Leo A. Daly Company of St. Louis delivered to the Joplin Land Clearance for Redevelopment Authority that summer contained a number of surprises:

- *To bring the hotel back to its original condition would cost $1.855 million, not including furnishings.*
- *Replacement value of the hotel was $5 million.*
- *The hotel, which once had 400 guest rooms, now had 329 as several had been combined to form suites and apartments.*
- *The hotel had only 32 permanent residents* [it once had a high of 100].
- *The hotel averaged only 30–45 guests per night, for a 22 percent occupancy rate.*
- *The copper cornices around the top of the building had badly deteriorated.*
- *The mechanical system of the 1908 portion had seen little updating of equipment and only a small amount of preventive maintenance.*
- *The original heating system had been given only minimal repair and little preventive maintenance. The hotel needed central air conditioning in place of the individual window units.*
- *The electrical system had not been updated since it was installed in 1908 and some of the equipment was worn out, broken, or corroded.*
- *The hotel did not meet fire code requirements.*

The Daly Company did offer four possible uses for the hotel, suggesting a combination of two or more of these options:

- *Demolish the 1908 portion and revitalize the remaining part, leaving around 140 guest rooms and ancillary facilities that would be more tailored to meet the needs of the downtown area. The space from the 1908 portion could be used for a new lobby, lounge, dining area, bar, meeting rooms, additional parking, a mechanical plant, and even a swimming pool.*
- *Convert the hotel into an apartment building, combining several of the rooms into suites, similar to what had already been done.*
- *Convert the hotel into housing for senior citizens, with the meeting rooms used for community space.*
- *Convert the hotel into an office building, including conference and public meeting space. The perimeter first-floor areas could be remodeled and used for commercial space.*

In an August 25, 1966 editorial, the *News Herald* summarized the hostelry's plight quite nicely: "It seems unlikely that anyone would undertake to restore the Connor to its complete original condition, because much of the business formerly attracted there when it was THE hotel in this part of the country has long since gone to the motels. It would be difficult to maintain a high rate of occupancy for 300 to 400 rooms in downtown Joplin, it seems to us."

In its final report issued in January 1967, the Daly Company increased the "rehabilitation" cost of the Connor to $2.445 million. But it had added the construction of an enclosed, four-story parking garage just north of the hotel on Main Street; conversion of the 1908 section to 78 apartments; and remodeling of the annex section to provide 134 rooms for continued hotel use. Although the report recommended remodeling of the lobby, it emphasized that the "handsome, curving marble staircase be retained—not only as an example of superb craftsmanship but also since it provides a ready access from street level to the second floor."

On the same day that the final Daly report was filed with the Joplin Land Clearance for Redevelopment Authority, Alberding attempted to land at the Joplin airport. A heavy fog sent his plane back to Tulsa, but the Alsonett owner returned that evening. The next morning, February 1, 1967, he signed papers selling the Connor for an estimated $500,000 to the Midwestern Land and Investment Company of Joplin and its thirty-six-year-old president, J.C. Vaughn.

On the surface, Cecil Vaughn appeared to be a self-made man who possessed the financial wherewithal to restore the Connor to its glory. At the age of twenty, he bought eighty acres of farmland in Miami County, Kansas. Seven years later, he traded that tract for a ranch in Bourbon County, Kansas, just north of Fort Scott. The ranch grew to 1,200 acres, which Vaughn used as collateral to purchase a nearby bank. He told a *Globe* reporter that he had large real estate holdings and investments in four states and South America. His portfolio also included mining, oil and life insurance stocks.

In a telling statement to the *Globe* reporter, Vaughn revealed how he was able to accumulate so much perceived wealth. "Credit is a great tool if you use it properly," he said. "I could never have done what I have without excellent financing and credit."

Vaughn and his twenty-seven-year-old wife, Martha, had moved to Joplin two years earlier because its airport could accommodate his extensive air travel and two private planes. The Vaughns had two children: a son, Timmy, born in 1962, and a daughter, Nancy, born in 1964. His first wife and a four-year-old son had died in a 1959 car-truck accident near Fort Scott, Kansas.

The financier became interested in buying the Connor several months earlier. "I had read about several other people wanting to buy it, and I had surveyed the possibilities and the area considerably," he told the *Globe*. "The building looked structurally sound and the location was excellent. I probably wouldn't have considered the purchase if it had been located on the south edge of Joplin. I figured Joplin's downtown district would grow to the north and [toward] the airport."

Alberding failed to conduct a due diligence study of Vaughn's financial situation. He accepted a promissory note in the amount of $111,802, while Vaughn assumed a $250,000 mortgage on the annex portion of the hotel held by Alberding and a $140,000 mortgage on the 1908 section still held by the Connor Investment Company. The only money that changed hands was a $5,000 cash option that Vaughn paid to Alberding in November 1966 when they agreed to the terms of the deal.

Vaughn said he had read the Daly report and found it useful but that he intended to continue operating the Connor as a hotel. He pledged a complete renovation, in excess of $500,000, starting with the exterior and the interior public facilities. After that, about one hundred rooms in the annex portion would be redecorated and refurnished. The new owner even mentioned converting the Roof Garden into a supper club/bar with a large, glassed-in area providing diners with panoramic views of the entire area.

In somewhat of a surprising move, Vaughn named a longtime portrait photographer as manager of the Connor. Paul Wingo had tried to purchase the hotel a few months earlier as part of a group called the Connor Park Plaza Redevelopment Corporation, which also included Ralph Nolan, Tom Connor's great-nephew.

The *Globe* called the sale "a landmark event for a great landmark" in an editorial titled "The Connor Lives On." The paper pointed out that the hotel was once again under local ownership and management, which would have a "favorable psychological impact" on the community. Finally, it praised the Joplin Land Clearance for Redevelopment Authority (JLCRA) for attempting to find a potential use for the hotel by authorizing the Daly study. "Razing the Connor in connection with downtown urban renewal rehabilitation was unthinkable; repulsive to even contemplate."

Urban renewal wasn't as kind to the Keystone Hotel. The JLCRA determined in 1967 that the architectural icon couldn't be rehabilitated and should be demolished. The *Globe* endorsed the decision in an editorial, claiming that the Keystone "had fallen into decay and deterioration" and wasn't as structurally sound or modern as the Connor.

The Keystone closed its doors for good on August 9, 1968. The owners, Ben and Morris Bormaster, received $110,000 from the JLCRA, which also paid an undisclosed amount for the demolition. By the summer of 1969, a wrecking ball had turned the one-time "palace hotel of the Southwest" into a pile of rubble.

The JLCRA sold the land where the hotel stood for $20,000 to Joseph and Sara Newman, who constructed a nondescript office building there and opened a Farm & Home Savings Association agency in 1970. The tract at Fourth and Virginia, the site of the four-story Keystone annex, was sold for $14,000 to the Jack Flournoy Insurance Agency and the Joplin Globe Publishing Company. Flournoy built an office building, and the *Globe* added a small parking lot.

Attempting to silence critics a year after the Keystone's demolition, the chairman of the JLCRA's board of commissioners said that the landmark was "nothing but a firetrap."

Through Wingo as his spokesman, Vaughn announced some grandiose plans for the Connor. The Roof Garden would be completely remodeled, with floor-to-ceiling plate glass windows providing diners and dancers a panoramic view of the city. The Empire Room would be tripled in size, able to accommodate 525 people for banquets and 800 or more for meetings. A million-dollar convention center would be built just north of the hotel, capable of serving 1,200 people at a banquet and seating 3,000 at a meeting. It would sit on top of a four-story parking garage and also have a swimming pool, a theater and several shops.

The new owner did produce some tangible results. The exterior of the sixty-year-old structure was sandblasted and cleaned. Shiny new stainless steel equipment had been installed in the kitchen. More than sixty rooms on the seventh and eighth floors in the annex section had been completely remodeled and modernized. There were plans to renovate the rooms on the upper floors of the older section and call them "Plaza" rooms because many of them contained views of the new Spiva Park and fountain at Fourth and Main.

Vaughn spent $80,000 alone on a new restaurant, dining room and cocktail lounge for the Connor. The strangely named VonConor Restaurant, with its dark-blue carpeting, claimed it had the best steaks in town and was open from 6:00 a.m. to 10:00 p.m. seven days a week. After dinner, guests could move over to the Blue Rendezvous cocktail lounge and listen to live music.

Perhaps sensing that his employer's house of cards might soon collapse, Wingo announced his resignation as Connor manager on January 1, 1968. "My first love has always been industrial photography and I have all along intended to return to that profession," he offered as his only explanation. Vaughn named his brother-in-law, Charles Alexander, as the new manager.

The Connor hosted its last major convention in June 1968, when nine hundred members of the Veterans of Foreign Wars and four hundred members of the Ladies Auxiliary came to Joplin for their state convention. For the first time in years, the hotel was sold out. Governor Warren Hearnes gave the keynote address at the Fox Theater, 415 Main, which city officials had considering purchasing for use as a convention center.

An announcement on October 1, 1968, turned the city on its ear once again. The thirty-five-year-old president of the Tulsa-based Community National Life Insurance Company declared that his company had purchased the Connor from Vaughn. "We are proud to be a part of the famous landmark," Jimmie J. Ryan told the *Globe*. "We consider it to be an excellent investment."

Vaughn was not around to answer any questions, and the purchase price was not disclosed at the time. The Community National Life Insurance Company did assume the $140,000 mortgage still owed to the Connor Investment Company. It was later revealed that Vaughn had not made any payments to Alberding either.

This 1968 postcard advertised the VonConor Restaurant and the Blue Rendezvous Cocktail Lounge on the back. *Joplin Historical Postcards/Joplin Public Library.*

Vaughn, who always avoided interviews whenever he could, never spoke publicly again. On Saturday, December 21, he, his wife and their two children boarded a twin-engine turboprop plane piloted by Roger Louden of Carthage at the Joplin airport. They were headed for a Christmas vacation in Florida, planning to stop in Tallahassee on their way to Miami. Not long into the flight, Louden radioed the Joplin tower that the plane was experiencing icing on the wings and they were about to turn back.

The plane crashed in a cow pasture about twelve miles north of Springfield, south of Pleasant Hope, and burst into flames. Greene County sheriff's deputies spotted at least two bodies among the wreckage, but the intense heat prevented immediate exploration after the flames had been extinguished. The deputies later said they could see the remains of only three people in the plane. It was believed that the two children were cremated in the blaze. The Vaughn family was buried at Ozark Memorial Park Cemetery in Joplin on Christmas Eve.

The Connor Investment Company, which was still owed $140,000 ($145,000 with interest) on the original section of the hotel, planned a foreclosure sale on May 20, 1969. After a meeting between CIC and Community National officials, the public sale was postponed indefinitely. A federal judge from Tulsa had sent the three interim managers he had appointed to replace Ryan (who had run into substantial legal problems) to Joplin a few days earlier to determine whether Community National should hold on to the hotel. "They were to see if there was any equity above the mortgages," Judge W. Lee Johnson told the *News Herald*. "They reported there probably was not; they found that the hotel itself is a losing proposition."

A "losing proposition" may have been an understatement. According to the three-man team, the Connor was losing between $7,000 and $8,000 per month, the air conditioning in the newly remodeled restaurant had broken down and would cost $7,000 to repair and the elevators also needed attention.

The Connor's reprieve lasted exactly one month. One of the three interim managers notified Connor manager L.R. Roush (Charles Alexander had resigned in March) on Thursday, June 19, that he was to close the hotel the next day. No guests were allowed to register that evening, the restaurant and cocktail lounge were locked and the Connor's seventy to eighty employees were informed that their employment was ending. The twenty-five permanent residents were also told to look for new housing.

Friday, June 20, was a surreal day at the Connor. For the first time in its sixty-one-year history, the hotel was closed. As employees waited in the darkened lobby for their final paychecks, Community National personnel were seen loading bottles of liquor from the hotel into the trunk of a limousine. A Joplin attorney representing Alberding notified the Jasper County sheriff, who in turn called Joplin police. The limousine was impounded, and the alcohol was returned to the hotel bar.

Among those losing their place of residence was a sixty-five-year-old woman who was in the process of closing her family's business that had been in operation for nearly seventy-two years. Josephine Rosenberg had lived at the Connor for almost twenty-five years and had been able to walk to Rosenberg's Shoe Store at 523 Main. Blanche McIntire, a public stenographer who had an office in the Connor for thirty-nine years, had to find a new place of business.

Fourth and Main became a rather lonely place in the evenings, according to the editor of the *News Herald*, after the downtown stores closed for the day. "Today, desolation is the best descriptive I can call up for this scene," Les Pearson wrote. "The Keystone is gone, the Connor is dark and gloomy, there's not even much traffic on the streets, except for whatever activity there is around the few remaining bars downtown."

The Connor faced one more public humiliation on Friday afternoon, August 15: a sheriff's sale at the Jasper County Courthouse in Joplin to determine if anyone wanted to own the money pit. Whoever purchased the hotel would be obligated to pay off the outstanding mortgages and back taxes, estimated at $630,000. A local man bid $25,000 on the stipulation that it had a clear title, which it clearly did not. Paul Wingo, the former manager, bid $75. Alberding bid $100 through his Joplin attorney and won the deed to the property. By obtaining the title, the attorney said that Alberding could now put the Connor back on the market.

Although Alberding said he had two potential buyers, the Connor's future remained precarious at best. As the decade drew to a close, most expected the hotel to meet the same fate as the Keystone: the wrecking ball. But one man was determined to save it. And his name wasn't Charles Alberding.

SAVE THE CONNOR

The Connor remained closed throughout 1970, although it was anything but a quiet year for the Grand Old Lady. Just six days into the new year, disaster struck. The Alsonett Hotel Company had neglected to drain the water storage tank on the top floor. When the temperature dropped, a pipe burst, sending cascades of water onto the floors below. The entire building was flooded, from top to bottom. Finally, someone noticed icicles over the Fourth Street entrance and had the water shut off.

Alsonett's Tulsa-based vice-president conducted negotiations with the Pentecostal Church of God on several occasions to buy the Connor. The PCG had made its world headquarters in Joplin since 1951, moving from Kansas City. The church had some interest in using it as a retirement center and for meeting space and even commissioned a feasibility study of the hotel.

In the end, though, the PCG purchased a block of property on Main Street between Second and Third Streets from the Joplin Land Clearance for Redevelopment Authority for $75,000. The church constructed a four-story building for its world headquarters in 1973, with Commerce Bank occupying the first floor and a portion of the basement. Two years later, it completed the fourteen-story Messenger Towers to provide apartments for senior citizens. At 145 feet tall, it surpassed the Connor by 15 feet as the tallest structure in Joplin.

Alberding continued to play a cat-and-mouse game with the county and the city over the back taxes Alsonett still owed. He offered to pay 60 percent of the $81,500 owed to the county in April 1970, but a Jasper County court turned him down. He owed city taxes of almost $42,000. Two weeks before the hotel went back on the auction block in August, Alberding ordered the sale of all of its furnishings, rugs, light fixtures, curtains and air conditioners. Even some door knobs, sink faucets and room doors were removed and sold.

Four days before the auction, the hotel magnate filed an injunction against the Jasper County collector to stop the sale for back taxes. A circuit court judge denied the petition the next day, saying that he assumed the county collector was correct in listing the description of the property for sale. When no one bid on the Connor, the collector announced that the county now owned the hotel for nonpayment of delinquent property taxes. Alberding's attorney, however, said because no bids were received, the Alsonett chain still owned it.

Ownership of the Connor would remain in dispute for another year. Meanwhile, the hotel continued to deteriorate. Although it had been closed to guests for two years, it was occupied by hundreds of pigeons, which nested on the roof and inside through the broken windows. Complaints from those who did business in the vicinity resulted in the city sending inmates to clean up the mess on the sidewalk in front.

Finally, on September 1, 1971, the Connor had new owners: Joplin real estate broker Burl Garvin and Roy Steele, owner of five Ben Franklin Stores in Joplin and Webb City. Garvin and Steele traveled to Tulsa to meet with Alberding and close the deal. Alberding signed a quitclaim deed, while the Joplin businessmen agreed to assume $375,000 worth of outstanding mortgages—including $130,000 still owed to the Connor Investment Company from a decade earlier—and pay county and city real estate taxes totaling nearly $116,000.

The new owners announced some ambitious plans for the hotel. They would spend $2.6 million on renovation and another $450,000 to build a four-story parking garage just to the north. "This would include converting the Main Street side, or old section of the hotel, into about 75 apartments, ranging up to three rooms, all with cooking facilities," they said. "We would enlarge some of the rooms in the new section, or Joplin Avenue side, to provide about 100 rooms for hotel guests."

About one week later, Garvin and Steele announced that they had changed the name of the hotel to the Connor Towers Apartments and Motor Hotel and had hired an architect/engineer to determine the feasibility and cost of enlarging the Empire Room by three thousand square feet. By November, the Garvin-Steele Development Company had hired a building superintendent

The London Shop opened in the Connor annex at the northeast corner of Fourth and Joplin in November 1971. *Post Art Library.*

and leased space to seven tenants in the Connor Towers including the London Shop, a men's clothing store.

As 1971 ended, the Connor appeared to have momentum finally on its side. The next year would be even better. Even the long-skeptical *Joplin Globe* agreed. "The story of this brick and mortar resurrection is surpassed only by the ambitious expectations now held for the Connor," the paper noted in a January 1972 editorial. "And as they unfold, assuming form and substance, there can be no denying that amazingly the Connor Hotel lives again."

Garvin and Steele were brimming with optimism, too, because a Hilton Hotels regional manager had visited the Connor three days earlier and led them to believe the chain might be interested in franchising the property. The manager described the hotel as "amazing" with "tremendous possibilities." He thought the lobby could be redecorated as something from the "Victorian era." He was also impressed by the number of meeting rooms and meeting space. He did have one suggestion: the hotel needed an indoor swimming pool, which could be incorporated into the planned parking garage.

Although Hilton Hotels chose not to franchise the Connor, Garvin and Steele were hopeful that the Connor Towers might be selected as the new home of the Jasper County Courthouse. The courthouse at Sixth and Pearl in Joplin had been destroyed by fire on June 23, 1972. The co-owners presented an architectural concept to the Jasper County Court within a week of the fire. The third floor of the hotel would be leased to the county for offices and courtrooms.

Before the summer was over, a ten-member citizens advisory committee appointed by the court recommended that a new courthouse be constructed at the site of the old one. The committee felt it made more sense to build a new one than to buy or lease an existing building and spend additional money renovating and maintaining it.

Garvin and Steele continued to ready the Connor Towers for occupancy. Garvin, in particular, was incensed that someone had taken the huge chandelier over the grand staircase while the hotel had been closed. Barney Allis had purchased the 1,200-pound fixture in 1928 when he built the annex. Garvin offered a $500 reward for the apprehension of the person or persons who "removed, sold, or bought" the ornate chandelier. When that failed to produce any results, he restored and installed a 152-bulb chandelier from the old Paramount Theater in Joplin.

The co-owners were pleased that the Joplin Historical Society selected the Connor lobby as the location for the city's ninety-ninth birthday celebration on March 26, 1972. A standing room–only crowd heard Margaret O'Connor, Tom Connor's great-niece, give a capsule history of the hotel titled "Hail to the Connor."

Garvin, Steele and newly appointed general manager Bill Grove hosted a "sneak preview" in October for a crowd of one thousand that included Missouri secretary of state James C. Kirkpatrick. They unveiled the new Red Flame Restaurant and Brass Rail Lounge featuring a black, red and gold color scheme and a newly redecorated lobby. Bunny Newton, president of the Downtown Joplin Association and owner of a jewelry store a block away, said that "downtown would never be the same without the Connor."

In November, a member of the Advisory Council on Historic Sites and Buildings inspected the Connor to determine if it belonged in the National Register of Historic Places. "The appearance of the hotel is dramatic...probably richer than it was in its original state," Dr. Billy Bob Lightfoot, a professor of history at Southwest Missouri State University, told the *Globe*. "It certainly was a grand hotel for its time and place and

The Joplin Historical Society celebrated the city's ninety-ninth birthday in the Connor lobby on March 26, 1972. *Joplin Historical & Mineral Museum.*

has been well kept and used. It seems to be a part of the landscape and a part of the character of the community." He said that he was most impressed with the marble staircase and the strong attachment the community had with the building.

The Advisory Council to the Missouri State Park Board unanimously approved the nomination of the Connor Towers Motor Hotel to the National Register at a level of "local significance" on December 9, 1972. On February 28, 1973, the Connor was officially added to the National Register. Garvin called it "the greatest thing that ever happened."

By this time, Garvin was under a tremendous amount of financial pressure. He had started selling stock in Connor Towers Inc. in 1972, but that raised only $75,000 from twenty-five investors. The equipment and furnishings alone for the new restaurant and cocktail lounge had cost him $90,000. There were mortgage, tax and insurance payments to make, and his employees expected to be paid. Garvin's partner, Roy Steele, who had grown tired of the money pit the Connor had become

Missouri secretary of state James C. Kirkpatrick (*fourth from left*) came to Joplin on October 11, 1972, to help place the Connor on the Joplin Historical Trail. Others are (*from left*) Dr. A. Paul Thompson, Barbara Johnson McKee, Roy Steele, Victor Hinton and Burl Garvin. *Post Art Library.*

and wanted to open more Ben Franklin Stores, asked that Garvin buy out his interests. So, as 1972 turned into 1973, the Connor had a sole owner again.

Garvin hoped to use the National Register designation to secure a $2 million loan and apply for federal funding to continue the renovation. He ran ads in the *Globe* seeking "large investors" to lend him $600,000, or less, for two years at 8 percent interest, but he got no takers. The only good news was that the Friends of St. Avips organization decided to have its eleventh annual ball in the lobby of the Connor on May 18.

By the end of the summer, Garvin had decided to forgo his plan of a motor hotel/apartment complex. Instead, the Connor would remodel space to accommodate 114 apartments—60 on the Main Street side and 54 in the annex. The ones in the annex would have kitchenettes, while those in the older portion would have three or four rooms. Prices would range from $150 to $400 per month, with all utilities paid except for telephone service.

Garvin had studied the Hotel Kansan in downtown Topeka, built in 1923–24 and converted to the Kansan Towers apartments after closing in 1968. The Kansan's two lower floors now contained offices and a bank, with the upper eight floors devoted to apartments. Garvin thought that the Kansan could be a model for the Connor, and he even planned to apply for a $2.5 million Federal Housing Administration loan. The loan included $750,000 for a five-story parking garage with runways to each floor of the building.

Then, abruptly, Garvin announced that he would be closing the Red Flame Restaurant and Brass Rail Lounge on Sunday, September 30, 1973. The retail shops and other tenants' offices would remain open. "I must honestly say that I do not feel that the facilities of the Connor that have been operating have received the cooperation of the downtown merchants to the extent that they should have enjoyed," he told the *Globe*. "I have never stopped trying to make this go. I feel that others in this community have not cooperated in furthering these efforts as they might have done. The importance of this prime corner and this mammoth facility exceed personal consideration."

Garvin said if fifteen to twenty people each would invest $5,000—either as short-term loans to his operating company or through stock purchase—he could continue operating the Connor. But currently, he could not afford to pay the restaurant and lounge's thirty-five employees their $9,000 monthly salaries. IRS agents paid him a visit two months later and padlocked the doors to the restaurant, kitchen and lounge, claiming that he owed nearly $19,000 worth of taxes withheld from his employees.

Harry Hoffman, who wrote a weekly column for the *Globe*, had become a fan of Garvin for his tireless efforts to keep the Connor open against all odds. "If the people who screamed to keep the hotel open would join the operating corporation and buy stock in the operation, maybe there would still be hopes for the hotel," he wrote on November 24, 1973. "It is badly needed in the downtown area as a meeting place and for the restaurant facilities. If the help is not forthcoming soon, the Connor doors may have closed for the final time."

The city had become concerned about the threat the building posed to passersby. A copper cornice had come loose from the top and crashed to the sidewalk, and several other cornices posed the same risk. Pigeons had been using the hollow, decorative cornices as nests, and the accumulation of pigeon manure and dead pigeons made them a threat to come down at any time. A city inspector found that another cornice had pulled away from the Connor and ordered that barricades be put up on both the Main Street and Fourth Street sidewalks. Garvin hired Ozark Engineering Company and its huge crane to remove the loose cornice and clean and reinstall the others.

One of the most respected men in the city addressed the "massive white elephant" at the northwest corner of Fourth and Main in his 1974 "State of the City" report to the Kiwanis Club. "With all due respect to some of our older, historically minded citizens, there is no way, in my opinion, that the Connor Towers can ever be restored to its former glory and profitability," said Bruce Adamson, president of the First National Bank and Trust Company. "The question then arises, what will become of it?"

That is the question that everyone asked for the next few years. Even Garvin didn't know the answer. He listed the property for sale in March for

$950,000, but there were no takers. He dropped the price to $875,000 by the end of 1974 and listed these features:

- *Exclusive Brass Rail Lounge, Red Flame Restaurant and Gold Dining Room*
- *Beautiful marble lobby and the famous Wine and Gold Empire Room with crystal chandeliers*
- *Over $200,000 value in stainless steel kitchen and service kitchen equipment, lounge, restaurant, dining room and ballroom fixtures*
- *Seating capacity of approximately 1,200 people at present time, with some improvements should seat 2,500 to 3,000 people*
- *Would be ideal for exclusive dinner theatre with approximately 500 to 600 seating capacity*

Garvin didn't mention the hotel rooms or apartments, which had not been used since the Connor closed in 1969 and were uninhabitable. Alberding had stripped nearly all of the guest rooms of ceiling lights, plumbing fixtures and heating facilities. The carpeting had been pulled up and stacked in various rooms of the building, which had created a fire hazard. The elevators also needed replacing or overhauling, as they didn't meet code requirements.

The owner allowed the Joplin Jaycees to use the third floor as a "Haunted Hotel" Halloween fundraiser in 1974. For one dollar, guests could visit "nine rooms of scary monsters, frightening ghosts, wicked witches and terrifying bodies." It was a huge success, drawing more than one thousand adults and children each of the last three nights. But it also demonstrated the extreme to which the Connor had been subjugated.

Garvin dropped the price to $795,000 in August 1975, but there was still little interest. His son, Phil, and Phil's brother-in-law reopened the Brass Rail Restaurant and Lounge in November, but other than that, it was an extremely quiet year. The Vickers plant held its annual Christmas party there, and for the third year in a row, the lobby was the scene of a New Year's Eve party hosted by the Garvin family. Things would pick up in 1976, however, and the Connor would once again be embroiled in the middle of controversy.

In January 1972, the Joplin City Council and the Joplin Public Library board agreed to build a new $1 million library. The Joplin Carnegie Library at Ninth and Wall was seventy years old; had run out of space; had seventeen steps leading up to the entrance, hampering the handicapped and the elderly; and didn't have a parking lot. The council and board

Public Library, Joplin, Mo.

Through a $40,000 donation by Andrew Carnegie, the Joplin Public Library opened at Ninth and Wall in 1902. *Joplin Historical Postcards/Joplin Public Library.*

decided that the new library would be located on the southeast corner of Fourth and Byers, which was once the location of Joplin High School and Joplin Junior College.

Construction on the new library wasn't scheduled to begin for a few years, as the funding had to be raised first. The city increased the tax levy for the library and contributed $750,000 from its budget over a three-year period. A $200,000 grant from the Missouri State Librarian's Office and funds squirreled away by the library staff brought the total close to the $1.3 million needed.

Just before construction was to begin, a core test drilling in May 1976 revealed an excessive amount of water in the middle section of the property at Fourth and Byers. A concrete support apron, about thirty inches thick, could be placed over the section but would cost at least $60,000. That wasn't in the budget, and the library board and city manager began looking elsewhere in the downtown area for a location.

It didn't take them long to conclude that the northwest corner of Fourth and Main would make an ideal home for a new library. The recently formed Downtown Redevelopment Corporation began negotiating with Garvin in August. On September 1, he agreed to take $259,000 for the Connor and another $91,000 for nearby buildings and parking lots.

As the Redevelopment Corporation began raising $450,000 for the purchase, demolition and relocation of existing tenants in the Connor, Garvin started having second thoughts about the razing of the hotel. He contacted the Department of Housing and Urban Development in October about the prospects of receiving block grants to provide housing for senior citizens in Connor apartments. He also asked HUD if the building could be torn down, given its placement in the National Register of Historic Places, and whether federal funds could then be used to build the new library.

Those questions would take months to answer. In the meantime, a Save the Connor Towers Building petition drive had started. The petition stated, in part:

> There have been published reports concerning plans to demolish the CONNOR TOWERS building, as part of downtown redevelopment. The vast majority of Joplin's citizens have not participated in discussions resulting in the published plans and do not share the published opinion that the CONNOR TOWERS building has outlived its usefulness. It is a Joplin historical landmark which cannot be replaced. Many progressive cities are preserving hotels of historical, social, cultural and commercial significance by adaptation to a residential-cultural center to meet the need of the community. As desirable as a new library building may be, it would be ironic that a landmark so important to the history and character of Joplin would be destroyed to make space for a library, as the purpose of a library includes preservation of the past.

Nearly 2,100 people signed the petition, including Garvin himself.

There were also bumper stickers encouraging everyone to SAVE THE CONNOR HOTEL. The Connor Hotel Restoration Fund was established to make needed repairs to prevent it from being condemned. "We're all in this fight together," said Betty L. Webb, president of the fund drive. "The building did not deteriorate overnight—it cannot be repaired overnight. The Connor has a 'new lease on life' now and we hope more people will take an optimistic look at the situation. Attitudes toward preserving attractive or historic buildings have shifted markedly. The Connor can be recycled into apartments or a business complex—with imagination and ingenuity the possibilities are limitless. The old hotel may have its problems but you wouldn't throw away the Liberty Bell just because it was cracked."

Some had plans for even more drastic action. One group proposed to surround the building by linking arms and forming a "Ring Around the

Connor." Another protestor allegedly planned to perch on the roof with a canteen and shotgun, threatening to "blast anyone who would harm the old landmark." It was also reported that area ministers were quoting Deuteronomy 19:14 from the pulpit: "Thou shalt not remove thy neighbour's landmark, which they of old time have set in thine inheritance."

Letters poured into the *Globe* protesting the decision to raze the Connor and offering alternatives. Dr. Winfred Post, a local ophthalmologist and civic leader, proposed using the entire ground floor of the hotel for the new library. "Elderly housing above, library and reading room service on the first floor, half a block of relaxation park, a small assembly group performance center, a show garden across the street, banking and drug and Social Security services within a step, all with attractive 'overlooks' to the 'Connor Square,'" he wrote on September 5, 1976.

A Joplin marriage and family counselor suggested removing the upper floors of the Connor and renovating the first and second floors for the new library. "It is within the two lower floors where most of the Connor's historic value lies; the magnificent entry, staircase, and ballroom," wrote Larry Burrows. "I hate to see it come under the wrecking ball without further consideration of how the solid and memorable parts of the structure may be a useful asset to Joplin. Once it is gone it will be nothing more than a collection of photographs and assorted nostalgia."

A history teacher at Parkwood High School in Joplin wondered why the new library couldn't be built on a vacant lot on a side street. "The Connor Hotel is the only remaining structure downtown that is of any artistic or historic significance," wrote Milo Harris. "What a shame to see it torn down to make way for a one-story library to replace another that is still perfectly adequate."

With the question still looming of whether the new library would still be eligible for federal funding if the Connor were to be torn down, city officials passed it on to Congressman Gene Taylor in December 1976. Taylor wrote to Gary Everhardt, director of the National Park Service, asking, "[C]an a building listed on the National Register be demolished?" It would take an entire year before that question could be answered.

The issue of whether to tear down the Connor divided the city. The city council, the Joplin Chamber of Commerce, the Downtown Redevelopment Corporation, the *Joplin Globe* and even the architect who prepared the application for the Connor to be added to the National Register all supported the action. William Cornwell said in a letter to Congressman Taylor that he viewed the demolition with mixed emotions, including the fact that the hotel's "classic design elements" would never be seen again. However, he said he considered the building dangerous and unsafe for those pedestrians walking below. "Unfortunately, I feel, it must yield to the wrecking bar and as much as I would like to see it remain as a landmark to Joplin's past, I'm afraid there is no one among us who can save it. It has become an 'albatross' around our neck, and some desperate measures need to be taken before it takes a life or injures someone or a number of the fine people of our community."

The *Globe* supported the razing, in part, because its president and general manager, Fred G. Hughes, was also the president of the chamber of commerce. The newspaper office was just a block away from the Connor, and the newsroom had a firsthand view of the hotel's deterioration. When *Globe* photographer Charles Snow took a picture of a tree sapling growing out of the brick wall on the eighth floor, the editors didn't hesitate to run the photo on the front page.

Seeing all the barricades constantly up at Fourth and Main, the *Globe* called the Connor a "serious safety and health hazard smack in the middle of town." The paper editorialized, "It's a safety hazard because of falling objects, certain to worsen as time goes on. It's a health hazard because the once gracious hotel, with the older section admittedly an architectural gem, has pathetically become the most imposing and spacious pigeon roost in the country."

On the other side were the Joplin Historical Society, the Jasper County Historical Society, the Webb City Historical Society, the Joplin chapter of the Daughters of the American Revolution and dozens of individuals who called themselves the "Friends of the Connor." One of the most outspoken was Bill Freeman, an eccentric real estate agent and collector who had once worked at the hotel. Freeman filed the 2,100 petition signatures with the city council, asked it to conduct a public vote on where the new library should be located and demanded an audit of the Redevelopment Corporation to make sure it had really raised the $450,000 to buy and demolish the building. The council informed Freeman that the library board would determine the location and that it could not order an audit of the corporation because it was a private entity.

The Save the Connor group found an ally in Dr. William J. Murtagh, the first "keeper" of the National Register of Historic Places. It was Murtagh who notified Garvin in 1973 that the Connor had been entered in the National Register. It was Murtagh whom Garvin contacted when he had second thoughts about the plan to demolish the hotel to build a library.

Others from Joplin began writing him as well, and the curator personally answered nearly every single letter.

Murtagh raised the ire of city officials and the *Globe* with his February 2, 1977 letter to Garvin. The "keeper" made it clear that he wanted the building preserved and rehabilitated. "The Connor Hotel is an extremely solid structure and we think that finding a way to adaptively use the building is a much more efficient use of time, money, and space than tearing it down and constructing a new building, particularly one of the size and shape of the proposed library," he wrote. Murtagh pointed out that the Connor could receive a historic preservation grant and that the City of Joplin could use community development block grant funds on its rehabilitation.

The *Globe* fired back, calling Murtagh "some faceless government staffer, 1,500 miles distant who probably has never been in Joplin." The paper accused him of dangling "another carrot on a stick" by mentioning new federal programs that encouraged the preservation of historic buildings.

Garvin, for his part, seemed to flip-flop between wanting the Connor preserved and torn down. In a letter to Missouri secretary of state James C. Kirkpatrick, he asked for the politician's help in removing the Connor from the National Register. He explained that he had tried every year since 1973 to obtain federal funding for the rehabilitation and that if the city condemned and demolished the building he would face a tax bill ranging from $300,000 to $400,000. "You have been in this building and know that I have spent several thousands of dollars on the first and second floors, and I feel that I do not have more money to invest in this building, at this time."

Garvin was also skeptical that the Redevelopment Corporation had raised the $450,000 to purchase and demolish the building. "They say they have solicited the funds to buy it, but I have no evidence of it," he wrote to Murtagh. Garvin said that he wanted to sell the property to release his liability but had no contract or appreciable earnest money, other than $200.

The Connor's ground-floor tenants were also moving out, which reduced his only source of revenue from the building. His son, Phil, had closed the Brass Rail Restaurant

Burl Garvin. *Neely Garvin Myers.*

and Lounge in February, claiming that its business had shriveled up after the Redevelopment Corporation announced that it had reached its $450,000 goal. Many customers assumed that the venue had closed as a result. Only a barbershop, a women's apparel store, a navy recruiter and a frame shop remained, but the latter would soon close.

As a result of Garvin's letter to Kirkpatrick, the director of the Missouri Department of Natural Resources decided to order an inspection of the Connor to arrive "at a proper solution to the present controversy." A state inspector for the DNR's Historic Preservation Office would tour the building and determine if it had lost its architectural integrity or if there had been an error in professional judgment during the 1972–73 nomination process.

Architectural historian Nancy Breme inspected the Connor on March 16, 1977. She allowed the news media to accompany her on the Garvin-led tour under the stipulation that they not ask any questions. In her site inspection report issued three weeks later, she made some interesting observations:

> The basement, a maze of rooms, bathrooms, and storage facilities, was currently serving as a "catch-all" for items no longer used. The enormous boilers of the original heating system had not [been] removed when a new heating and cooling system was installed.
>
> The lobby and main hallways retained much of their original integrity. The frescoes on the walls of the lobby and landing of the grand staircase were in good condition. There were several cracks in the lobby's tile floor and a few missing tiles.
>
> The Empire Room was in excellent condition and retained much of its original integrity.
>
> The original integrity of the third and sixth floors was good, as intact wall ornamentation remained in nearly all rooms. Dead pigeons were found in several rooms. Few window panes were broken, but some screens were missing. The water damage from the 1970 pipe freezing was most severe on the sixth floor. [Breme did not inspect the seventh and eighth floors.]
>
> Most of the original integrity of the exterior remained. Only canopies over doorways and new store windows altered the building's original appearance.

Breme concluded, "Based on my observations, I do not believe that the Connor Towers Motor Hotel has been sufficiently altered since placement on the National Register of Historic Places on February 28, 1973 to warrant its removal....The present lack of maintenance and upkeep of the building on the exterior and interior is cause for concern, but proper care and adequate funds should correct the problem."

Garvin's reaction? "I think it is a good report," he told the *Globe*.

The city continued to put some subtle pressure on the owner, sending him a certified notice on May 25 that a "nuisance" existed at Fourth and Main: the accumulation of pigeon manure on the sidewalks. "We also respectfully request that you discontinue the practice of just sweeping the manure and debris off into the street gutter as this is not a satisfactory approach to the problem," the notice stated. Garvin was given ten days to abate the nuisance.

At least two Joplin residents had recommended the year before that the new library be located within the existing Connor building. That idea was supported in the summer of 1977 by the regional environmental officer for the Department of Health, Education and Welfare, who had been commissioned by the Advisory Council on Historic Preservation to conduct an in-depth study. The report recommended using the basement for book stacks, the first floor for reading areas and stacks and the mezzanine level for reading areas.

"It is our hope after exploring this fine building that it can be recycled— if not for a library then for some other viable function," wrote William Henderson. "We must insure that, in the redevelopment of the city, we protect its significant heritage so that it does not indiscriminately destroy what earlier citizens have created, found beautiful and cherished."

The HEW officer, in fact, thought the Connor would be perfect as the home of the new library and became almost giddy at the prospect:

> *The ornamental tile floor, the walls with wainscots and decorative panels in molded plaster, the unique ornamental plaster ceilings, and most specifically, the immense, imposing round marble columns and grand marble staircase and marble balustrade of the circular opening into the mezzanine above—all create a grandeur that is most appropriate for a public/civic experience....The adaptive reuse of these elements offers a rare opportunity for an institution, but particularly a library whose very foundation is in history and cultural resources.*

Henderson said that remodeling the Connor into a library would cost less than constructing a new building, but replacing the entire mechanical system would cost slightly more. The building would need new plumbing, wiring, heating and air conditioning systems and a fire protection system.

The Advisory Council on Historic Preservation agreed with the HEW conclusion that the new library should be located in the Connor. The decision didn't sit well with the library board or the *Globe*. Head librarian Margaret Hader claimed that it would require a tripling of the library staff and the installation of an elevator.

H. Lang Rogers, *Globe* publisher and executive editor, didn't mask his feelings: "Putting the library into the present Connor Hotel building makes about as much sense as it would to put the Missouri Southern stadium there. There is absolutely no compatibility, the cost would be prohibitive, and we would still have a dirty and unacceptable eyesore in the center of downtown Joplin."

The Advisory Council on Historic Preservation in Washington, D.C., agreed to come to Joplin in November 1977 for a public hearing. Joe Hough, the Advisory Council's Midwest representative, and Orval Henderson, the assistant state historic preservation officer in Missouri, were told by the library board why putting the new library in the Connor was a bad idea: mainly, it would cost $96,000 more per year to staff three floors rather than a single one.

The architect hired to design the new library building said that it would cost nearly $2.5 million to remodel the basement, first floor and mezzanine level and that this figure did not include fixing the upper seven floors to bring them up to code. He estimated the total price to be between $3.5 million and $3.8 million. The state librarian, Charles O'Halloran, who had traveled from Jefferson City, emphasized, "Never put a library in a historic building."

The mayor was just as adamant. "If you're going to continue the Connor as a historic building, then give us enough money to fix it up," William Mauldin implored. "Otherwise let us tear it down." Because no agreement was reached after a two-hour-plus meeting, Hough and Henderson agreed to remain in town to continue discussions the next day.

That closed meeting turned out to be a two-and-a-half-hour bargaining session with the "city fathers and the Joplin economic elite," the *St. Louis Post-Dispatch* reported a few months later. "The outcome suggests that horse trading remains a living art in southwest Missouri." The article accused Hough and Henderson of acquiescing to the city by agreeing to a deal that all but signed the Connor's death warrant.

The "decision package" reached on November 4, 1977, included these provisions:

- If someone wanted to save the Grand Old Lady, they would have to come up with a bona fide preservation plan and

$750,000 in cash or certified check—$300,000 to purchase the building and pay off the mortgage and $450,000 to bring the building into compliance with city codes and stabilize the exterior. The *Post-Dispatch* thought that the $450,000 seemed "a bit on the high side: $20,000 per floor for cleaning up pigeon droppings, for instance."

- The deadline for submitting the plan and money would be February 18, 1978, which was thirty days after the formal ratification of the agreement.
- The Missouri State Historic Preservation officer and the City of Joplin would determine whether the preservation plan was feasible.
- In the absence of a feasible plan, the state and federal preservation agencies would withdraw all objections to the demolition, and the Connor would be removed from the National Register after it had been demolished.
- The city would salvage and preserve several architectural features of the Connor, including wall murals from the lobby, segments of the copper roof balustrade, copper brackets from the cornice, the lion-face keystone over the main entrance, decorative frieze panels over windows and segments of the marble balustrade from the lobby. These features would be incorporated into the interior, exterior or landscaping of the new Joplin Public Library or donated to the Joplin Historical Society.

One month later, HEW and city officials signed an agreement to remove the Connor from the National Register, allow federal funds to be used for the construction of the new library and nominate the existing library at Ninth and Wall to the National Register. The Joplin Carnegie Library was added in 1979.

One of Joplin's most beloved citizens then decided to take matters into his own hands in an eleventh-hour attempt to save the Connor. Vernon Sigars, who would be nicknamed "Mr. Joplin" a few years later and have a viaduct named after him, formed the Southwest Missouri Heritage Foundation just two weeks before the deadline that had been set in the agreement. "Many of our most colorful and significant landmarks have been felled in the past few years," he told the *Globe*. "We feel it would be a cause of disgrace and great shame to the citizens of Joplin if the Connor is the first National Register building to be destroyed in Missouri, which will be the case if the Connor is demolished."

Sigars invited the statewide Preservation Task Force to come to Joplin to tour the hotel and discuss alternatives to the demolition. The meeting attracted a developer, Jack Oliver, of Overland Park, Kansas, who quickly put together a proposal that would turn the Connor into at least eighty apartments for senior citizens. Sigars, seventy-seven years old at the time, declared that housing for senior citizens was Joplin's greatest need. The proposal was contingent on receiving funding from the Missouri Housing Development Commission and the U.S. Department of Housing and Urban Development.

At first, the city council refused to consider the renovation plan from Sigars and Oliver, voting unanimously to reject it because the men didn't have the required $750,000 in cash. Sigars argued that they had $250,000 in cash, plus pledges for additional funds, and asked for an opportunity to discuss all the options. The navy veteran of World War I and army veteran of World War II then got into a verbal sparring match with City Manager James Berzina. Sigars likened tearing down the Connor to "cutting off your foot to cure a corn." Berzina retorted that saving the hotel was "like saving a dinosaur."

The *Globe* supported the council's decision, saying that it had "acted responsibly." In an editorial headlined "Connor Epitaph," the paper said that time had run out for the hotel. "Plans should now go swiftly forward for demolition of the cherished but deplorably decadent hulk of a building in making way for a new Joplin Public Library."

Robert Townsend, the acting director of the Missouri Department of Natural Resources and the state historic preservation officer, urged the council to reconsider and give Sigars and Oliver a hearing. The city agreed to the meeting, with the mayor claiming that it would make the final decision on accepting or rejecting the proposal.

The council called a special meeting at noon on Thursday, March 2, 1978, to determine the Connor's fate. A major winter storm in northern Missouri prevented Oliver and a member of the State Historic Preservation Office from attending. Sigars, left alone to defend the proposal, chose to say little, as he was still stinging from his rebuff at the previous meeting. This session lasted only twenty minutes and mainly consisted of the city presenting opinions from various officials that the chances of receiving state and federal funds for the project were minimal. Berzina said that he had asked Oliver if the developer would be willing to put some of his own money "up front" to guarantee the project and that the answer was no. The council then voted eight to zero to deny Oliver's proposal.

Garvin, who mailed the *Globe* clippings to Murtagh in Washington, D.C., seemed to have changed his mind again about what should happen to the Connor. "It seems as though the city is going to have their way about the demolition of this building and doing away with one of the best buildings in Joplin," he wrote. Garvin pointed out that he was paying $2,500 per month on the mortgage and a monthly insurance premium of $1,260 and expressed his frustration with the Downtown Redevelopment Corporation, which was paying him $500 per month as an option on the building but nothing toward its maintenance.

The January 28, 1978 fire at the historic Coates House Hotel in Kansas City inspired Garvin to write a letter to President Jimmy Carter. The deadliest fire in Kansas City history, it killed twenty and left more than one hundred residents homeless. In his letter, Garvin said it was regrettable that fireproof buildings such as the Connor were being demolished while numerous old buildings—including nine in Joplin—were allowed to remain to be a "fire trap threat to the safety of mankind." He pointed out that the Connor was all steel and concrete but was "being sacrificed for the whim of the 'modern buffs' with financing provided by our federal government."

Garvin urged Carter to do something about the country replacing its heritage symbols with concrete block buildings and parking lots. "It is time we concentrate federal spending for preservation instead of destruction," he concluded.

Meanwhile, Townsend had concluded that while Oliver's plan was "reasonable and probably workable," it was not feasible due to the lack of adequate financing. "For a number of years plans and proposals for re-use of the Connor Hotel have been presented but financing was always lacking, as is now the case," he wrote to Robert Garvey Jr., executive director of the Advisory Council on Historic Preservation. And as Townsend pointed out, Oliver was not willing to put his own money into the project.

Townsend recommended that the provisions of the November 4, 1977 agreement be implemented, which included the demolition of the Connor.

In June, following eight hours of negotiations by seven attorneys and sixteen others, the final warranty deed was transferred from the Connor Towers Development Company to the Library Landholders Inc. The Garvin family received $286,316.70 but owed $2,443.68 in prorated taxes for 1978. The city council spent another $97,000 in Community Development funds

Above: Barricades surround the Connor a few days before its scheduled demolition. *Greg Holmes.*

Left: A final view of the Connor's iconic grand staircase. *Greg Holmes.*

to acquire other properties, including one from Garvin, north of the Connor to make room for the new library.

Preparations were made for the demolition of the Connor on Sunday, November 12, 1978. In a presentation to the Joplin Rotary Club just three days before, the owner of Dyke Explosive Service Company of Tulsa dispelled the widespread belief that the hotel was structurally sound. "It is in rotten condition," Jim Redyke said. He said that the steel beams in the upper floors were rusty and the concrete columns were "flaky."

Redyke said that four or five of his employees would tape about three hundred explosive charges to the steel framework in the older portion of the hotel and place two hundred pounds of dynamite in holes in the steel-reinforced concrete pillars of the annex section. About 90 percent of the charges would be placed in the basement and the rest on the first floor. A rapid series of blasts ignited by electrical charges would bring the Connor down in fourteen or fifteen seconds. "I anticipate no problems with the implosion, but we are taking every precaution," he noted.

The city health director and his staff planned to spend the day before demolition watering down the top floor to prevent the spread of a fungus found in pigeon droppings. Tests had found the fungus on the top floor, making it necessary to soak the area so the dust created by the explosion wouldn't spread the organisms. City workers also removed hundreds of dead pigeons earlier in the week.

Those who had advocated the razing of the Connor were looking forward to the Sunday morning demolition. The general contractor for the project, the Coy Blagg Wrecking Company of Tulsa, had invited several city residents to a dance at the Ramada Inn the night before and to a breakfast that morning to celebrate. KOAM-TV had scheduled a live remote beginning at 7:45 a.m., with the explosives set to be detonated shortly after eight o'clock.

A TRAGIC ENDING

Twenty-four hours before the scheduled demolition, Alfred Summers and Frederick Coe III were in the basement of the Connor Hotel using acetylene torches to cut notches into the steel beams. One floor up, Thomas Oakes was doing the same thing. Later in the day, explosive charges would be placed in the notches. It was Saturday morning, November 11, 1978.

Sandra Williams was with her twelve-year-old son, David, taking some final pictures of the Grand Old Lady. She heard a "loud cracking sound" and then saw the top of the older section of the hotel sway toward Main Street "like a serpent." The middle of the east wall then bowed out and came back. The building then collapsed, sending out a blinding cloud of dust and debris. The fifty-year-old annex remained standing. It was 9:15 a.m.

It took the rest of the day to determine exactly how many members of the demolition crew were in the Connor when it collapsed. Early news reports said that four or five had been trapped inside. When the *Globe* went to press late Saturday night, it said at least three, possibly five, were believed missing. None had been publicly identified.

Rescue crews and volunteers converged on the Connor almost immediately. Heavy equipment operators from local construction firms cleared debris away. The Missouri National Guard brought in large dump trucks to haul it away. Nearly every fire department surrounding Joplin sent men to help dig in the rubble. The Empire District Electric Company installed floodlights so that rescue operations could continue around the

Above: Downtown Joplin was the focus of the nation's attention for five days in November 1978. *Greg Holmes.*

Left: The Connor annex still standing after the collapse. *Greg Holmes.*

clock. The Red Cross, the Joplin chapter of the Veterans of Foreign Wars and the Salvation Army provided food and drink to the volunteers.

Hundreds of people waited behind barricades at Fourth and Main, waiting and praying for some sign of life. Others were glued to their radios and TVs, hoping for some good news.

A coal mining company from Pennsylvania flew in a special listening device used in mining disasters. The clearing away of debris was halted as the sound wave detector was put into place. It was capable of hearing a human heartbeat, but there was only silence.

On Sunday, the identities of the three missing workers were released. Alfred Summers was thirty-one years old, from Joplin, an air force veteran of the Vietnam War and an employee of the A&A Construction Company. Frederick Coe III was twenty-nine; from Topeka, Kansas; and a 1970 graduate of Washburn University. Thomas Oakes was forty-five; from Jenks, Oklahoma; a navy veteran of the Korean War; and an employee of Coy Blagg Wrecking.

Summers had a wife, Patricia, and a young stepson, Tommy. Coe had a wife, Debra, and two sons, Frederick IV, four, and Zachary, two. Oakes had a wife, Joyce, and a six-year-old son, Bo.

Debra Coe was at the Connor when the building collapsed. "She was on the job site standing near the back of a pickup truck where they were getting the explosives ready," recalled her son, Fred Patton.* "She heard a loud noise and looked toward the hotel to see it fall. They all began to run away from the hotel as they didn't know what was happening."

Fred Coe wasn't even supposed to be in Joplin that day. He worked for his wife's family business—Vince Bahm Demolition in Topeka—and had met Jim Redyke, the owner of Dyke Explosive Service Company, the week before in Kansas City. Debra wanted to watch the Connor come down, so the couple headed to Joplin and Fred was hired for the day by Redyke.

A man in the St. Louis suburb of Florissant had been following the national news coverage all weekend. Raymond Garner, head of the Law Enforcement K-9 Search & Rescue, called the Joplin Police Department and offered his services. The JPD verified his credentials with the Missouri Highway Patrol before inviting him to come.

---

* When Debra Coe married Terry Patton in 1985, Patton adopted Fred and Zachary. In 1988, eleven-year-old Zachary was hit and killed by a car. Fred Patton graduated from Washburn and the University of Kansas School of Law and was elected to the Kansas House of Representatives in 2015.

Sir Joel, a six-year-old German shepherd, and trainer Raymond Garner (*second from right*) assist searchers in going through the rubble. *Joplin Historical & Mineral Museum.*

Garner and his six-year-old German shepherd, Sir Joel, flew to Joplin and began digging in the rubble around 7:30 p.m. Monday—fifty-eight hours into the rescue effort. Sir Joel, imported from Germany at the age of six months, had been used for a variety of jobs, ranging from detecting illegal drugs to finding escaped prisoners. The canine sniffed around for several hours, finding "some positive information," according to Garner, just before midnight.

As Monday turned into Tuesday, many of the volunteers began to doubt that anyone could still be alive. It had been three full days since the collapse. Would there even be any air left for someone to breathe? The fact that several live pigeons had been found in air pockets brought some encouragement. Whenever rescue workers found an air pocket, they would holler "Hey" down into it, but would hear only an echo in response.

Garner and Sir Joel resumed their search on Tuesday morning. The dog seemed interested in one particular area, sniffing at it and then pawing at it. The crew intensified their search in the general vicinity. When Harold Snyder, general superintendent of Snyder Brothers Construction, found another air pocket and shouted "Hey," he was startled to hear someone shout "Hey" back.

Alfred Summers had been found in the northeast section of the basement. A cheer arose. He had been buried alive for seventy-seven hours. "Boys, I'm ready to get out of here," he said. It wouldn't be that easy though. Summers was under two slabs of concrete that had fallen together and created a cavity eighteen to twenty-four inches high and thirty feet long. He had tried crawling out on his stomach, banging on pipes and calling out for help.

Workers carefully used shovels and even their hands to remove the rubble, being especially careful not to cause the concrete slab to crush him. A garden hose was passed through a small hole to provide him water, and later he was given an oxygen mask connected to a tank on the surface. Two hours after the discovery, Southwestern Bell in Joplin established a telephone hookup with Summers so that he could communicate while being extricated. He hadn't realized that the entire building had collapsed on him—he thought only the first floor had fallen.

Joplin Globe reporter Marta Churchwell persuaded a Webb City firefighter to take a co-worker's automatic camera and snap this picture of Alfred Summers as he was being pulled out of the rubble. The photo ran in hundreds of newspapers across the country the next day. *From the* Joplin Globe.

Summers was finally freed at 7:34 p.m. Tuesday—eighty-two and a half hours after the collapse. A crowd of about two hundred that included Missouri lieutenant governor William Phelps applauded and cheered as he was carried out. An ambulance took him to St. John's Medical Center, where he was listed in satisfactory condition with three broken ribs and a fractured pelvis.

"If you've never witnessed a miracle, you have tonight," Joplin police chief Larry Tennis told a reporter.

In an exclusive interview from his hospital bed with Paul Stevens, the Associated Press correspondent from Wichita, Summers vividly described his ordeal:

> *Everything was dark. I never lost consciousness; I can remember almost everything that happened. I found a piece of pipe and started pounding and yelling, but I couldn't hear anything. It was dark all the time down there. I never heard anything until Tuesday.*
>
> *I couldn't tell how big a space I was in. It was dark. I never could sit up. There was just room to lay on my side or on my back. I kept moving around, looking around for an opening, but I could never find one.*
>
> *I have a wife and one child, but I didn't have time to think about a lot of things other than finding a way to get out. It seemed like I was down there for two days. I got awfully hungry and thirsty, but the hunger didn't bother me much. I was getting awfully thirsty, though. I dozed now and then, but I was never able to sleep very long.*
>
> *I did an awful lot of praying. I prayed to Jesus, because he's the only one I knew could get me out of this. I'm not much of a religious man, but if anyone could get me out alive, it had to be Jesus.*

Buoyed by the discovery of Summers, rescue workers continued their "inch-by-inch" search on Wednesday. The *Globe*'s Wally Kennedy reported that with more than three-fourths of the rubble cleared away, officials were claiming that Coe and Oakes could be found at any time. Rescuers zeroed in on three promising sites near where Summers had been found. Sonar testing continued, as did the use of Sir Joel.

Coe and Oakes were found on Thursday: Coe at 7:05 a.m. about fifty-five to sixty feet from Summers's location and Oakes at 1:53 p.m. in the center of the basement near the first-floor stairwell. Both had died instantly of head and chest injuries. The rescue and recovery operation was called off, and the National Guard was deactivated.

Demolition of the Connor annex on November 19, 1978. *From the* Joplin Globe.

Summers was dismissed from St. John's Medical Center at noon on Saturday, having spent only four nights in the hospital. His pelvic fracture turned out not to be as serious as first believed, and he was able to get around on crutches after going home.

On Sunday morning, November 19, exactly one week after the Connor was supposed to be blown up, the nine-story annex was demolished in only six seconds. Redyke used about 110 pounds of dynamite to bring down the 140-room structure.

The finger-pointing over who was responsible for the disaster began soon after the bodies of Coe and Oakes had been removed. Henry Parker, field superintendent for Coy Blagg Wrecking, blamed it on the decision to use explosives instead of a wrecking ball. "The only difference between using explosives and the machine-and-ball method, the conventional method, it [explosives] does it quicker, but it's a thousand-to-one more dangerous," Parker told Paul Stevens of the Associated Press.

Company owner Coy Blagg acknowledged that it was his decision to use explosives. But he was only trying to save the Library Landholders Inc. some money. "I told Mr. Parker I would shoot the building," he said. "This was a not-for-profit organization I was doing it for and I felt obligated to get it done the cheapest way. Using explosives was the cheapest way."

The Occupational Safety and Health Administration began an on-site investigation into the cause of the building's collapse. "We know what happened," OSHA spokesman Warren Hargreaves said six days after the disaster. "They apparently cut enough columns that the building wouldn't support itself anymore. The question is was something being done to ensure that too many columns weren't cut. The building was self-supporting for 70 years, and then it wasn't anymore on Saturday morning. The only thing that would cause that is if too many columns were cut."

OSHA fined the prime contractor, Coy Blagg Wrecking, $5,400 and the subcontractor in charge of explosives, Dyke Explosive, $4,500 for "willful" safety violations. Specifically, OSHA said that an engineering survey should have been made to determine the condition of the framing, floors, walls and the possibility of collapse of any portion of the building. Blagg did not comment, and Redyke, the owner of Dyke, said that he would appeal the citation. "If you read the definition of a survey, I made one," Redyke said.

Blagg and Redyke did appeal, and OSHA later reduced the violations from "willful" to "serious" and the fines to $1,000.

Both the Oakes and Coe families filed lawsuits in 1979. Joyce and Bo Oakes, the widow and the son, sought $8 million from Dyke Explosive, alleging that the demolition firm committed seven acts of negligence. The lawsuit claimed that Dyke was "oppressive, malicious and grossly negligent and exhibiting a total disregard for the life and safety of the deceased." They settled for $100,000 and $25,000, respectively.

The Coe family asked for $2 million in actual damages and $10 million in punitive damages from Dyke, Coy Blagg Wrecking and Joplin's Library Land Holding Corporation. Debra Coe received $100,000 and her two sons $20,000 each in their settlement.

Summers received only a $30,000 settlement. Ten years after the collapse, he was making $8 per hour working for his brother-in-law at Crane Roofing Company and drawing unemployment during the winter months. He died in 2012 at the age of sixty-four.

Construction on the new library finally began in April 1980. The project had been delayed for nearly a year by $63,000 in mechanic's liens filed against the property by local contractors who assisted in rescue and cleanup operations but had never been paid. R.E. Smith Construction Company of Joplin, which submitted the low bid of $1.6 million, completed the thirty-two-thousand-square-foot building in January 1981.

The new Joplin Public Library opened on the footprint of the Connor Hotel on May 8, 1981. It took another fourteen years for the two carved

The two caryatids were returned "home" to the new Joplin Public Library in 1995. *Greg Holmes.*

panels and two caryatids to be returned "home" from the Joplin Regional Airport, where they had been in storage since 1978. Carolyn Trout, head librarian from 1987 to 2006, oversaw the installation of the stone friezes on the outside of the children's wing library addition and the caryatids inside.

"We felt like the Connor was still with us in many ways," Trout said. "I had a dozen or more people tell me over the years they had never been in the new library because they were so upset the Connor had been torn down or the old Carnegie library abandoned."

Missouri Southern State University rescued the carved stone lion's head that stood over the Connor entrance from the weeds at the Joplin airport. The university mounted it on a brick display that had been erected in front

The Joplin Public Library occupied the location of the former Connor Hotel from 1981 to 2017. *From the* Joplin Globe.

of the Spiva Art Center and unveiled it during homecoming in 1985. Five years earlier, MSSU had named a large gathering space on the third floor of the Billingsly Student Center the Connor Ballroom.

After thirty-six years at the Connor Hotel location, the Joplin Public Library moved to a new, larger building at Twentieth and Connecticut in May 2017. One of the city's redevelopment projects following the May 2011 Joplin tornado, it was funded in part by a $20 million grant from the U.S. Department of Commerce's Economic Development Administration.

The MSSU Foundation acquired the former public library building in March 2018 and announced plans to turn it into a downtown campus. The foundation plans to include a tribute to the Connor when it is remodeled for use by academic programs.

Hundreds of people still remember where they were when the Connor Hotel collapsed on November 11, 1978. It is one of the most popular topics on the Facebook "You Know You're from Joplin If…" discussion group. Until the 2011 Joplin tornado, it was the single most defining moment in the city's history.

BIBLIOGRAPHY

Newspapers

Albany Capital
Atop the Connor Bulletin
Baxter Springs (KS) Daily Citizen
Camden (AR) News
Carthage Press
Chanute (KS) Daily Tribune
Chariton (IA) Herald Patriot
Chillicothe Constitution-Tribune
Coffeyville (KS) Morning News
Columbia Missourian
El Paso (TX) Herald-Post
Fort Scott (KS) Daily Tribune
The Hotel World: The Hotel and Travelers Journal
Independence (KS) Daily Reporter
Indianapolis (IN) News
Jefferson City Daily Capital News
Joplin Daily Globe
Joplin Evening Times
Joplin Globe
Joplin Morning Tribune

Joplin News Herald
Joplin Sunday Globe
Kansas City Star
Kansas City Times
Miami (OK) Daily News Record
Moberly Evening Democrat
Nashville Tennessean
Neosho Daily Democrat
Neosho Daily News
Neosho Times
Palmyra Spectator
Pittsburg (KS) Daily Headlight
Salt Lake City (UT) Telegram
Sedalia Democrat
Sedalia Democrat-Sentinel
Sedalia Weekly Sentinel
Springfield Leader and Press
Springfield News Leader
St. Louis Post-Dispatch
St. Louis Star and Times
Tampa Bay (FL) Times
Washington (D.C.) Post
Webb City Register
Wichita (KS) Daily Times
Wilson (NC) Daily Times

Secondary Sources

Ashford, Carolyn, to Burl Garvin, February 23, 1977. The National Archives Catalog. https://catalog.archives.gov/OpaAPI/media/63819503/content/electronic-records/rg-079/NPS_MO/73001042.pdf.

Breme, Nancy. "Connor Towers Motor Hotel Site Inspection March 16, 1977." April 4, 1977. The National Archives Catalog. https://catalog.archives.gov/OpaAPI/media/63819503/content/electronic-records/rg-079/NPS_MO/73001042.pdf.

Burrough, Bryan. *Public Enemies: America's Greatest Crime Wave and the Birth of the FBI, 1933–34.* New York: Penguin Books, 2004.

Cook, Kevin. *Titanic Thompson: The Man Who Bet on Everything.* New York: W.W. Norton & Company, 2011.

Cornwell, William, to Congressman Gene Taylor, January 10, 1977. The National Archives Catalog. https://catalog.archives.gov/OpaAPI/media/63819503/content/electronic-records/rg-079/NPS_MO/73001042.pdf.

Crawford, Joan, to Steve Howard, April 24, 1957. Posted by Marolyn Howard Higgins to "You Know You're from Joplin If…" Facebook group, January 29, 2013.

Draper, William R., and Mabel Draper. *Old Grubstake Days in Joplin*. Girard, KS: Haldeman-Julius Publications, 1946.

Ferrell, Robert H., ed. *Dear Bess: The Letters from Harry to Bess Truman, 1910–1959*. Columbia: University of Missouri Press, 1998.

Fowler, Richard B. "Frank J. Dean." *Leaders in Our Town*. Kansas City, MO: Burd and Fletcher, 1952.

Garvin, Burl, to President Jimmy Carter, March 10, 1978. The National Archives Catalog. https://catalog.archives.gov/OpaAPI/media/63819503/content/electronic-records/rg-079/NPS_MO/73001042.pdf.

Garvin, Burl, to William J. Murtagh, March 3, 1978. The National Archives Catalog. https://catalog.archives.gov/OpaAPI/media/63819503/content/electronic-records/rg-079/NPS_MO/73001042.pdf.

Grigonis, Richard. "The Flatiron Building, New York City." Interesting American, January 3, 2011. interestingamerican.com.

Groth, Paul. *Living Downtown: The History of Residential Hotels in the United States*. Berkeley: University of California Press, 1994.

Historic-Memphis. "The Peabody Hotel." http://historic-memphis.com.

Historic Menger Hotel. "Welcome to Our Historic Hotel in San Antonio." https://www.mengerhotel.com.

Historic Preservation Alliance. "Then and Now: Allis Hotel." http://www.historicpreservationalliance.com.

Kansas Memory. "Hotel Kansan, Topeka, Kansas." https://www.kansasmemory.org.

Lulay, Gail. *Nelson Eddy, America's Favorite Baritone: An Authorized Biographical Tribute*. San Jose, CA: Authors Choice Press, 2000.

Mangan, J.A., and Andrew Ritchie, eds. *Ethnicity, Sport, Identify: Struggles for Status*. New York: Routledge, 2005.

Marshall, Rex, and Harry Guinn to Buel Fisher, January 7, 1977. The National Archives Catalog. https://catalog.archives.gov/OpaAPI/media/63819503/content/electronic-records/rg-079/NPS_MO/73001042.pdf.

McCamant, John Mortimer. *Mack's Barbers' Guide*. Ogden, UT: Wasatch Printing Company, 1908.

Memorandum of Agreement Between Joplin Connor Hotel and U.S. Department of Health, Education, and Welfare, January 13, 1978. The National Archives Catalog. https://catalog.archives.gov/OpaAPI/media/63819503/content/electronic-records/rg-079/NPS_MO/73001042.pdf.

Minutes of Special Council Meeting, Joplin, Missouri, March 2, 1978. The National Archives Catalog. https://catalog.archives.gov/OpaAPI/media/63819503/content/electronic-records/rg-079/NPS_MO/73001042.pdf.

Morris, David. *Royal Navy Search and Rescue: A Centenary Celebration*. Stroud, Gloucestershire, ENG: Amberley Publishing, 2015.

Murtagh, William J., to Burl Garvin, February 2, 1977. The National Archives Catalog. https://catalog.archives.gov/OpaAPI/media/63819503/content/electronic-records/rg-079/NPS_MO/73001042.pdf.

National Register of Historic Places Inventory, Nomination Form, Connor Towers Motor Hotel, September 15, 1972. https://catalog.archives.gov/OpaAPI/media/63819503/content/electronic-records/rg-079/NPS_MO/73001042.pdf.

National Transportation Safety Board. "Airframe Icing, MU-2, near Pleasant Hope, Missouri." https://www.fss.aero/accident-reports/dvdfiles/US/1968-12-21-US.pdf.

North, F.A., ed. *The History of Jasper County, Missouri*. Des Moines, IA: Mills & Company, 1883.

Osmundson, Theodore. *Roof Gardens: History, Design, and Construction*. New York: W.W. Norton & Company, 1999.

Popper, Joe. "The Hotelier: The Legend of Barney Allis." *Kansas City Star Magazine* (April 30, 1989).

Ranker. "The Best Detroit Tigers of All Time." https://www.ranker.com.

Robinson, Earl, and J.C. Hounschell, official notice, to Burl Garvin, May 25, 1977. The National Archives Catalog. https://catalog.archives.gov/OpaAPI/media/63819503/content/electronic-records/rg-079/NPS_MO/73001042.pdf.

Serena, Katie. "Robert Wadlow—The Tragically Short Life of the World's Tallest Man." All That's Interesting. https://allthatsinteresting.com.

Sharoff, Robert. *American City: St. Louis Architecture: Three Centuries of Classic Design*. Victoria, Australia: Images Publishing Group, 2010.

Shields, David S. *The Culinarians: Lives and Careers from the First Age of American Fine Dining*. Chicago: University of Chicago Press, 2017.

Sigars, Vernon, to Robert Townsend and William Mauldin, February 16, 1978. The National Archives Catalog. https://catalog.archives.gov/OpaAPI/media/63819503/content/electronic-records/rg-079/NPS_MO/73001042.pdf.

Smith, Jacob. *The Thrill Makers: Celebrity, Masculinity, and Stunt Performance*. Berkeley: University of California Press, 2012.

Tallman, Richard. "Vance Randolph Interviewed." *Missouri Folklore Society Journal* (2004).

Tankersley, Ted R., to Buel Fisher, January 7, 1977. The National Archives Catalog. https://catalog.archives.gov/OpaAPI/media/63819503/content/electronic-records/rg-079/NPS_MO/73001042.pdf.

Taylor, Gene, to Gary Everhardt, December 3, 1976. The National Archives Catalog. https://catalog.archives.gov/OpaAPI/media/63819503/content/electronic-records/rg-079/NPS_MO/73001042.pdf.

Teaford, Jon C. *The Metropolitan Revolution: The Rise of Post-Urban America*. New York: Columbia University Press, 2006.

Thomson, David. *The New Biographical Dictionary of Film*. 6th ed. New York: Alfred A. Knopf, 2014.

Townsend, Robert, to Robert Garvey Jr., March 8, 1978. The National Archives Catalog. https://catalog.archives.gov/OpaAPI/media/63819503/content/electronic-records/rg-079/NPS_MO/73001042.pdf.

Trout, Carolyn. Interview by author, February 11, 2020.

Turkel, Stanley. *Built to Last: 100+ Year-Old-Hotels East of the Mississippi*. Bloomington, IN: AuthorHouse, 2013.

Wallis, Michael. *Pretty Boy: The Life and Times and Charles Arthur Floyd*. New York: W.W. Norton & Company, 1992.

Wallower, E.Z. *Reminiscences of E.Z. Wallower*. Harrisburg, PA, 1941.

Weinstat, Hertzel, and Bert Wechsler. *Dear Rogue: A Biography of the American Baritone Lawrence Tibbett*. Portland, OR: Amadeus Press, 1996.

White, J.T., ed. *The National Cyclopaedia of American Biography*. New York: James T. White & Company, 1960.

Whitney, Carrie Westlake. *Kansas City, Missouri: Its History and Its People, 1808–1908*. Vol. 3. Chicago: S.J. Clarke Publishing Company, 1908.

INDEX

ABOUT THE AUTHOR

Chad Stebbins is a professor of journalism and director of the Institute of International Studies at Missouri Southern State University. He is also the executive director of the International Society of Weekly Newspaper Editors. Stebbins is the author of *All the News Is Fit to Print: Profile of a Country Editor*, published by the University of Missouri Press in 1998.

Visit us at
www.historypress.com
··